DK Pocket Genius

AMERICAN
SIGN
LANGUAGE

200 ESSENTIAL WORDS AND PHRASES

CONTENTS

04 American Sign Language
06 Signs and sentences
08 Using ASL

10 EVERYDAY WORDS

12 Me / You / Two of us / We / They
14 Big / Small / More / Less
16 Please / Sorry / Yes / Excuse me / No
18 Stop / Ask / Need / Cannot
20 Like / Help / Don't like
22 Good / Better / Bad
24 What / When / Who / Why
26 Which / Where / How / There
28 How are you? / Fine / So-so
30 Hello / My name is... / What is your name?
32 Nice to meet you. / Thank you
34 Are you deaf? / I'm hearing. / What is the sign for...?
36 What time is it? / It's 7:30.

38 HOME AND FAMILY

40 Mom / Dad / Grandpa / Grandma
42 Sister / Aunt / Brother / Uncle
44 Pet / Cat / Dog / Bird
46 Bedroom / Window / Door
48 TV / Phone / Computer / Tablet

50 You come to my house.
52 How do I get there?
54 Can I go to the bathroom, please? / Close the window.
56 Where is the kitchen? / It's through there. / I don't know.

58 FEELINGS

60 Feel / Happy / Sad / Scared
62 Jealous / Surprised / Angry / Bored
64 Excited / Love / Proud / Curious / Embarrassed
66 Frustrated / Disgusted / Nervous / Tired
68 Hot / Hurt / Cold / Safe
70 I'm nervous about the doctor's appointment.
72 You look excited. / It's my birthday tomorrow.
74 Do you like surprise parties?

76 FOOD AND DRINK

78 Hungry / Full / Thirsty / Eat
80 Breakfast / Dinner / Lunch / Drink / Water
82 Ice cream / Cookie / Cereal / Cheese / Yogurt
84 What is your favorite food? / I love pizza.
86 I'll make you a sandwich.
88 I want an apple and an orange.

Senior Editor Neha Ruth Samuel
Project Editor Bipasha Roy
Editorial Team Janashree Singha,
Suchismita Banerjee, Pranay Mathur,
Deeksha Miglani, Kritika Gupta
Art Editors Anastasia Baliyan, Prateek Maurya
Illustrators Abhimanyu Adhikari, Diya Varma
US Senior Editor Jennette ElNaggar
US Executive Editor Lori Cates Hand
Deputy Managing Art Editor Shreya Anand
Managing Editor Kingshuk Ghoshal
Managing Art Editor Govind Mittal
DTP Coordinator Vishal Bhatia
Production Editor Anita Yadav

Production Controller Joss Moore
Jacket Designer Govind Mittal
DK India Creative Head Malavika Talukder
Publisher Andrew Macintyre
Art Director Mabel Chan
Managing Director Sarah Larter

Consultant Patrick Rosenburg
Contributor Lizzie Munsey

First American Edition, 2025
Published in the United States by DK Publishing,
a division of Penguin Random House LLC
1745 Broadway, 20th Floor, New York, NY 10019

Copyright © 2025 Dorling Kindersley Limited
25 26 27 28 29 10 9 8 7 6 5 4 3 2 1
001–345767–Mar/2025

90 I am allergic to nuts.
92 Would you like a drink? / A glass of water, please.

94 SCHOOL AND ACTIVITIES

96 Read / School / Write / Book
98 English / Science / History / Math
100 Teacher / Class / Test
102 Homework / Study / Gym / Coach / Student
104 Win / Play / Lose / Game
106 Football / Soccer / Hockey / Baseball
108 Walking / Biking / Dancing / Skateboarding
110 Movie / Music / Video games / Travel / Painting
112 My favorite class is math.
114 Have you done your homework? / Not yet.
116 Do you play basketball? / Sometimes.

118 NATURE

120 Outdoors / Mountain / River / Ocean
122 Tree / Forest / Flower / Butterfly
124 Sky / Star / Moon / Sun
126 Rain / Cloud / Snow / Wind
128 Is it very sunny outside?

130 It's dark and windy this evening.
132 Summer is my favorite season.

134 ACTION AND DESCRIPTIVE WORDS

136 Come / Go / Move / Stay
138 Fall / Jump / Run / Climb
140 Catch / Give / Throw / Take
142 Listen / Shout / Tell / Whisper
144 Forget / Know / Think / Guess / Remember
146 Understand / Misunderstand / Agree / Disagree
148 Can I help you? / Can you feed the cat?
150 Let's go to the ballpark.
152 Are you going swimming today?
154 I walk the dog before school.
156 ASL alphabet
158 ASL numbers
160 Glossary / Acknowledgments

LEFT HAND DOMINANT
This symbol means that the illustrated character is left-handed—their left hand is their dominant hand.

A catalog record for this book is available from the Library of Congress.
ISBN 978-0-5939-6431-6

DK books are available at special discounts when purchased in bulk for sales promotions, premiums, fund-raising, or educational use.

For details, contact:
DK Publishing Special Markets,
1745 Broadway, 20th Floor, New York, NY 10019
SpecialSales@dk.com

Printed and bound in China
www.dk.com

This book was made with Forest Stewardship Council™ certified paper—one small step in DK's commitment to a sustainable future. Learn more at **www.dk.com/uk/ information/sustainability**

FSC
MIX
Paper | Supporting
responsible forestry
FSC® C018179

American Sign Language

A sign language uses hand movements to express words. American Sign Language (ASL) is used by many Deaf and hard of hearing people around the world, by their hearing friends and families, and by other hearing people.

Signing words

Like other languages, sign languages may have differences in vocabulary or grammar or even in the way you sign a word. The ASL sign for the word "mom" is different from the sign in British sign language (BSL).

Mom
ASL

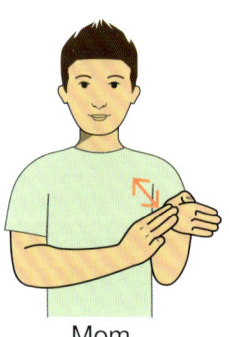

Mom
BSL

Sign languages

Many sign languages are used around the world. Some of them are unique to communities or countries. Among the most-used sign languages are Chinese, Indo-Pakistani, Russian, Brazilian, and Spanish. ASL and BSL are two different sign languages for signing English.

Many elements

ASL signs are made of: handshape, movement, location, palm orientation, and facial expression. Together these elements form a word.

Naming the hands

The hand you use the most is called your dominant hand—it can be your left or right, just as with writing. Your other hand is called your nondominant hand, and it forms a handshape only during two-handed signs.

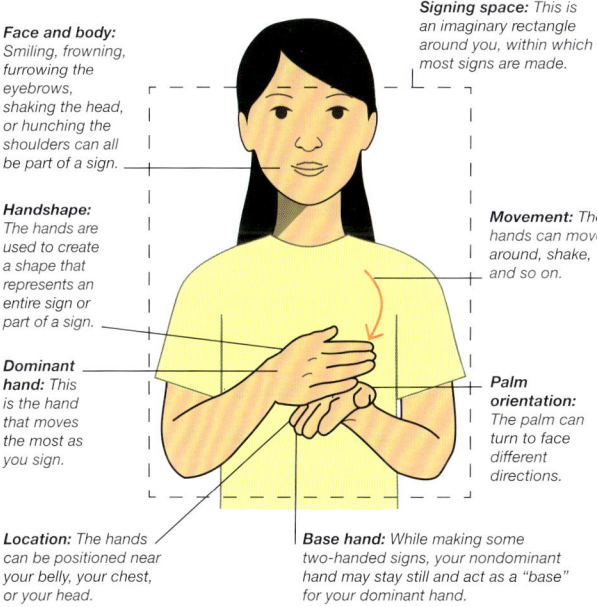

Face and body: *Smiling, frowning, furrowing the eyebrows, shaking the head, or hunching the shoulders can all be part of a sign.*

Signing space: *This is an imaginary rectangle around you, within which most signs are made.*

Handshape: *The hands are used to create a shape that represents an entire sign or part of a sign.*

Movement: *The hands can move around, shake, and so on.*

Dominant hand: *This is the hand that moves the most as you sign.*

Palm orientation: *The palm can turn to face different directions.*

Location: *The hands can be positioned near your belly, your chest, or your head.*

Base hand: *While making some two-handed signs, your nondominant hand may stay still and act as a "base" for your dominant hand.*

Signs and sentences

American sign language has its own vocabulary and grammar, which are not always the same as those you will know from spoken English.

Pronouns

You can use the index finger of your dominant hand to point to people, instead of using their names.

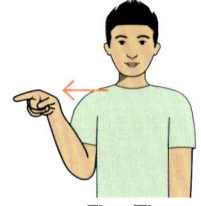

They/Them

Making a sentence

A sentence can be expressed in different word orders in ASL. Facial expression may be important in making sentences.

What is your name?

English

YOUR + NAME + WHAT

OR

WHAT + YOUR + NAME

OR

YOU + NAME

ASL

Connecting verbs

In ASL, connecting verbs are part of the signs, so words such as "are" and "is" are not used. To say "How are you?," we would sign "How You?"

How   **You**

Asking questions

Furrowing your eyebrows or raising them can change a sentence into a question. You could also use the sign for "?" at the end of the sentence.

Raise your eyebrows.

Furrow your eyebrows.

Crook and straighten the index finger of your dominant hand, twice.

Raised eyebrows

Furrowed eyebrows

?

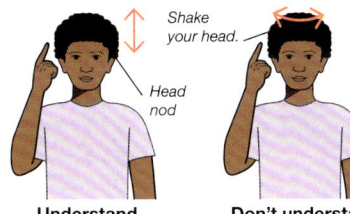

Shake your head.

Head nod

Understand

Don't understand

Changing the meaning

Shaking your head while signing shows that you mean the exact opposite to the sign. Here, a nod turned into a head shake changes the meaning.

FINGERSPELLING

If you're not sure of the sign for a word, you can spell it out one letter at a time by fingerspelling (see pages 156–157).

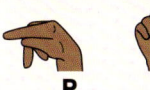

P

A

R

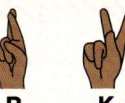

K

Using ASL

Sign languages bring Deaf and hearing people together, allowing them to talk to each other. Using ASL is more than just signing, though—there are important guidelines that everyone needs to follow.

Who uses ASL?

Deaf and hard of hearing people vary in their ability to hear or speak. Some of them may choose to lipread, while others sign using ASL because it is a visual language. Some neurodiverse people may also choose to use ASL. Many hearing people use ASL to communicate with those who are unable to hear or speak.

Tell me ...

Sometimes people use both ASL and a spoken language to communicate.

VARIATIONS IN SIGNS

There can be different ways of signing the same thing in ASL, depending on where you live and whether you're with friends or need to use more formal language. This is similar to dialects in the English language in different parts of the US.

Doing it right

The Deaf community has etiquette about how to interact, just like the hearing community does. Here are some things to keep in mind when communicating.

Get attention first
Make sure you have the person's attention. If they are looking away from you, tap them lightly on the shoulder.

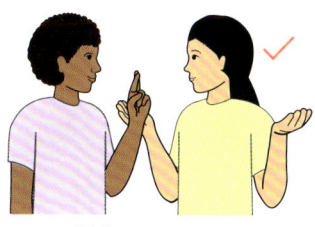

Make eye contact
It's rude to break eye contact with the person you're communicating with, or to look away during a conversation.

Do not cover your mouth
Speak clearly, and don't cover your mouth or chew gum. Those who lipread need to see your mouth movements.

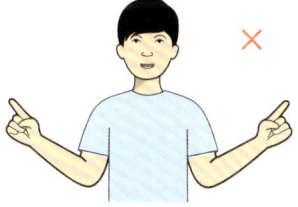

Avoid large movements
Don't exaggerate your body and mouth movements, and don't speak extra loudly or stand too close.

Chapter 1

EVERYDAY WORDS

Here are some basic words you'll need to know for many everyday conversations, including "hello," "thank you," "yes," and "what." Find out also how to introduce yourself to someone in ASL and to say that you're hearing.

◀ ASL sign for number 1

Me

Point the index finger of your dominant hand at your chest, with the rest of your fingers curled into a fist.

You

Point the index finger of your dominant hand at the person you are speaking to, with the rest of your fingers folded in.

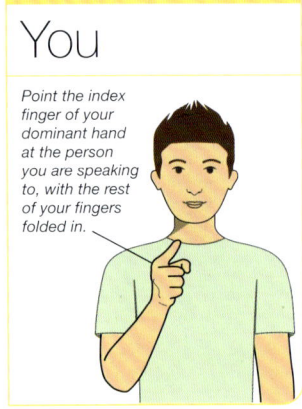

We

1 Point the index finger of your dominant hand at the shoulder nearest to it.

2 Move your hand in a semicircular motion to point the index finger at the shoulder opposite it.

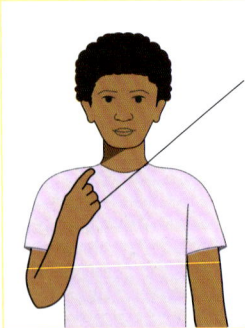

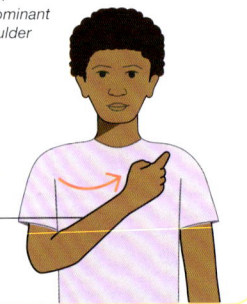

Two of us

This sign is a version of "we," where you are referring to yourself and the person you are talking to.

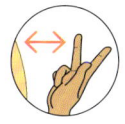

Hold your middle finger closer to your chest.

1 *Place your dominant hand in front of your chest, with the palm facing the body.*

2 *Stick out the index and middle fingers, with the rest of the fingers folded in. Bend the wrist forward and backward a few times.*

They

1 *Point the index finger of your dominant hand forward, with the rest of the fingers folded in.*

2 *Rotate your arm sideways away from your body, pointing with your index finger.*

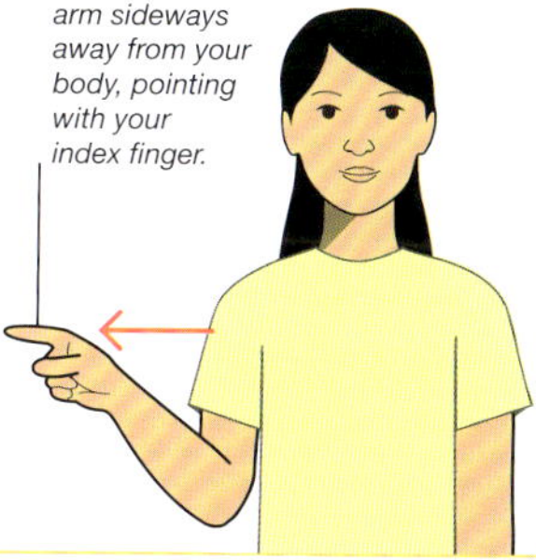

Big

1 *Hold your hands out in front of your chest, with the palms open, relaxed, and facing each other.*

2 *Move your hands sideways and away from each other.*

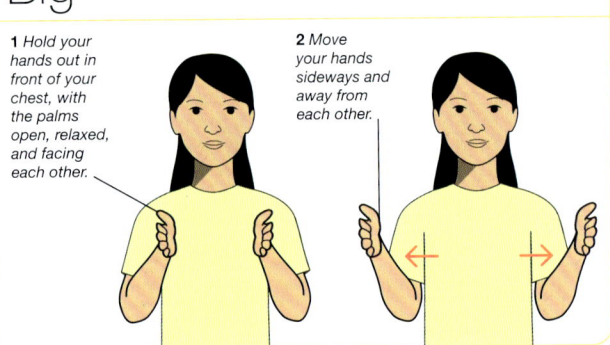

More

1 *Pinch together the fingers and thumb of each hand, and then point them at each other in front of you.*

2 *Bring your hands together so they touch at the fingertips.*

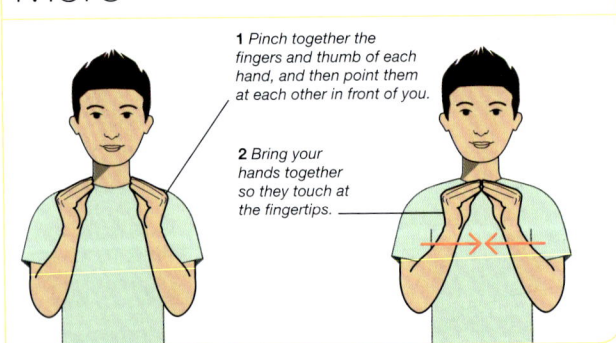

Small

Left hand dominant

1 *Hold your hands out in front of your chest, with the palms open, relaxed, and facing each other.*

2 *Move your hands toward each other and then away again, several times.*

Squint your eyes

3 *Mouth the letter "L."*

4 *Shrink your shoulders a little.*

Less

2 *Bend your dominant hand in half and hold it in front of your chin, facing downward.*

1 *Hold your nondominant hand near your chest, with the palm relaxed and facing up.*

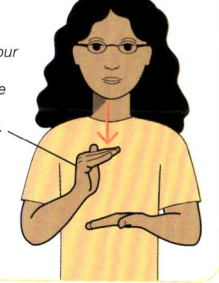

3 *Lower your dominant hand to the middle of your chest.*

Please

Left hand
dominant

*Hold your
dominant hand
to your chest,
with the fingers
together and
the thumb out.
Move it in a
circular motion.*

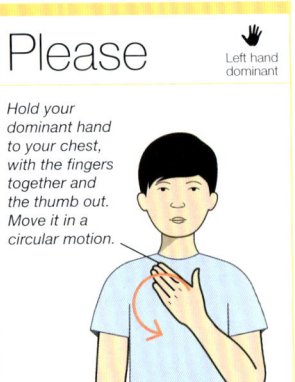

Sorry

*Keep a sad
expression on
your face.*

*Make a fist
with your
dominant
hand, and
move it in a
circle across
your chest.*

Excuse me

1 *Hold your
nondominant
hand in front
of you, with
the fingers
together and
palm facing up.*

2 *Bend your dominant hand
in half, and touch the tips
of your fingers to the
palm of the other hand.*

3 *Move your dominant
hand across the palm of
your other hand, twice.*

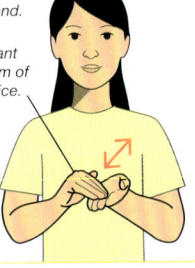

Yes

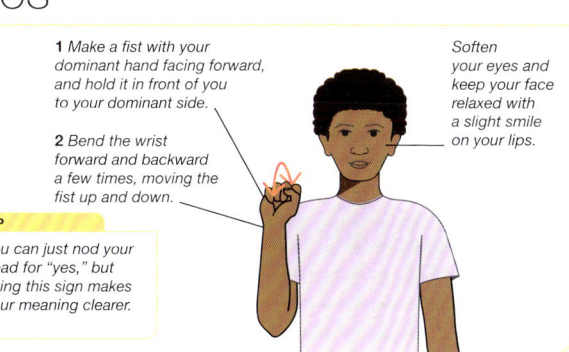

1 *Make a fist with your dominant hand facing forward, and hold it in front of you to your dominant side.*

2 *Bend the wrist forward and backward a few times, moving the fist up and down.*

Soften your eyes and keep your face relaxed with a slight smile on your lips.

TIP

You can just nod your head for "yes," but using this sign makes your meaning clearer.

No

1 *Fold in the ring and little fingers of your dominant hand and extend the other fingers and thumb.*

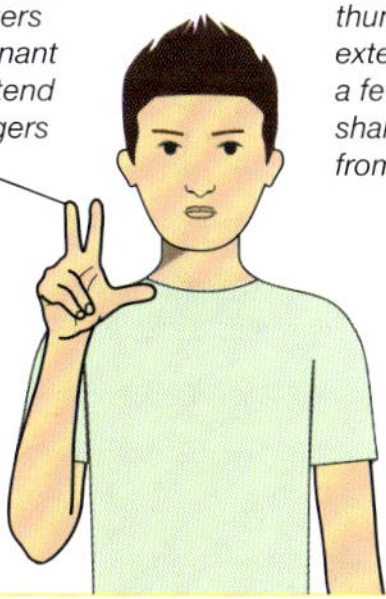

2 *Touch your thumb to the extended fingers a few times, while shaking your head from side to side.*

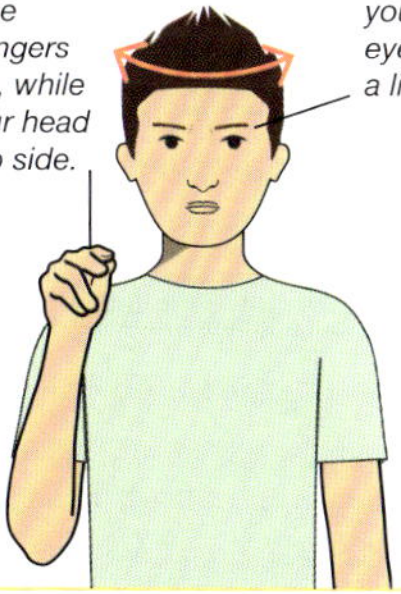

Furrow your eyebrows a little.

Stop

2 *Hold your dominant hand in front of your chest, with the palm flat and facing in and fingers held together.*

1 *Place your nondominant hand flat in front of your belly, with the palm facing up.*

3 *Bring your dominant hand down to touch your other hand.*

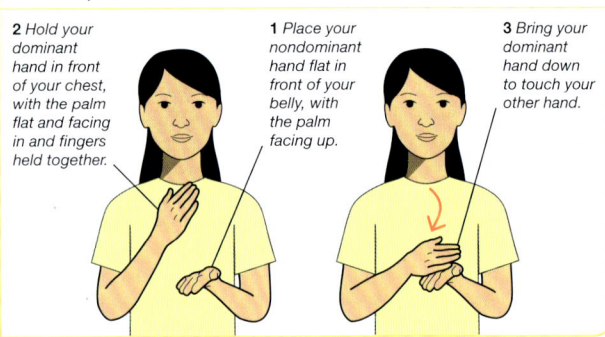

Need

1 *Bring your dominant hand in front of your chest. Crook the index finger of this hand, and curl the other fingers into a fist.*

2 *Bend your wrist downward so that the knuckle of your crooked finger is pointing forward.*

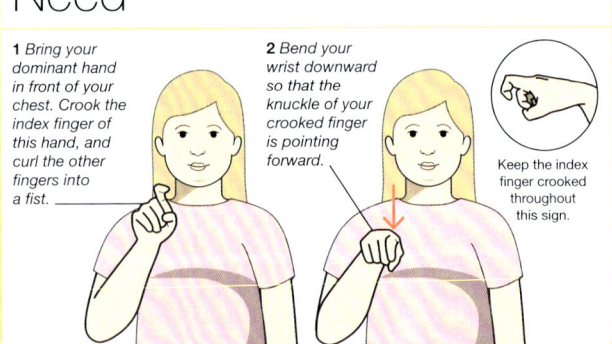

Keep the index finger crooked throughout this sign.

Ask

Use this sign when making a request. You can also fingerspell "X" to sign this word.

3 *Turn your hands so that they point upward, and touch the palms together.*

2 *Touch the fingertips of both hands together.*

1 *Bring your hands together, palms facing each other in front of your chest.*

Cannot

1 *Make a fist with your dominant hand facing downward, with the index finger pointing out.*

Shake your head while signing.

2 *Place your nondominant hand below the other one. Curl it into a fist, with the index finger pointing to your dominant side.*

3 *Quickly lower your dominant hand so that the index finger hits the index finger of the other hand.*

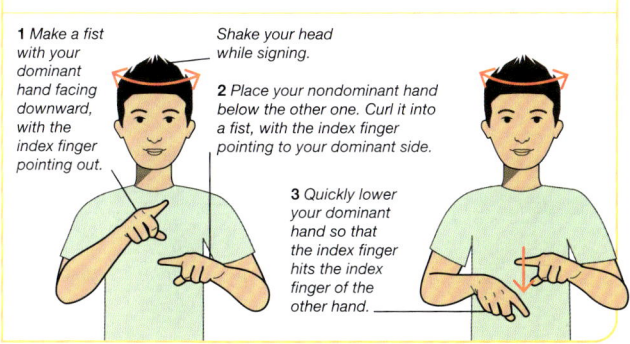

Like

Left hand
dominant

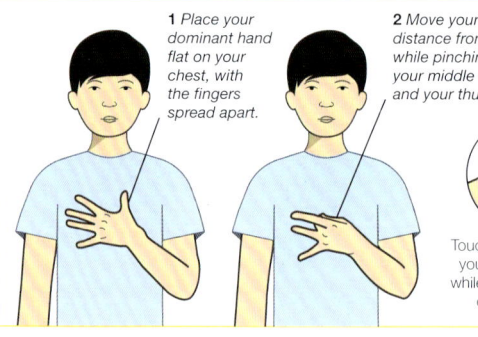

1 *Place your dominant hand flat on your chest, with the fingers spread apart.*

2 *Move your hand a short distance from your chest, while pinching together your middle finger and your thumb.*

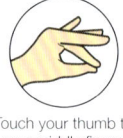

Touch your thumb to your middle finger, while sticking out the other fingers.

Don't like

The sign for "don't like" is similar to "like" but with an extra step. You will need to purse your lips and wrinkle your nose a little, to make it clear that you "don't like."

1 *Place your dominant hand flat on your chest, with the fingers apart.*

Help

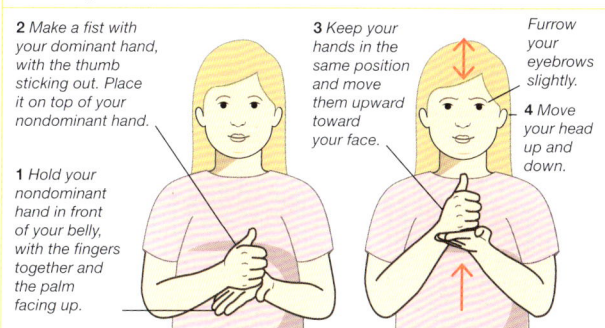

2 *Make a fist with your dominant hand, with the thumb sticking out. Place it on top of your nondominant hand.*

1 *Hold your nondominant hand in front of your belly, with the fingers together and the palm facing up.*

3 *Keep your hands in the same position and move them upward toward your face.*

Furrow your eyebrows slightly.

4 *Move your head up and down.*

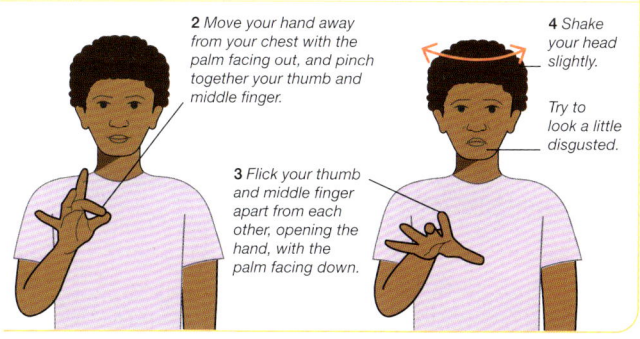

2 *Move your hand away from your chest with the palm facing out, and pinch together your thumb and middle finger.*

3 *Flick your thumb and middle finger apart from each other, opening the hand, with the palm facing down.*

4 *Shake your head slightly.*

Try to look a little disgusted.

Good

In many places, people use just their dominant hand to sign "good," keeping their other hand down.

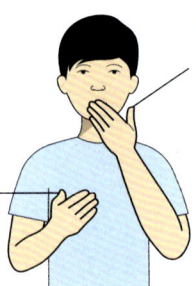

2 *Touch the fingers of your dominant hand to your mouth.*

1 *Hold your nondominant hand flat in front of you, with the palm facing you.*

Better

Signs for some words in ASL combine movements from related words. For example, "better" starts with a hand movement that looks similar to "good."

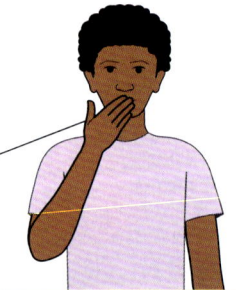

1 *Touch your mouth with the fingers of your dominant hand, with the thumb sticking out and the palm flat and facing you.*

Left hand
dominant

3 *Move your dominant hand down so that the back of it touches the palm of your other hand.*

Smile slightly.

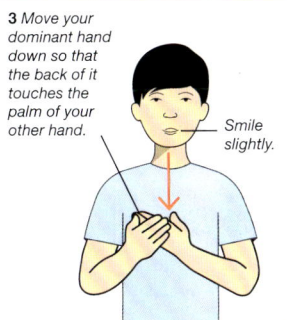

Bad

Furrow your eyebrows and turn down the corners of your mouth to show a slight frown.

2 *Touch your mouth with the fingers of your dominant hand.*

1 *Hold your nondominant hand flat in front of you, with the palm facing up.*

2 *Move the hand outward to the side, while curling the fingers into a fist and sticking out the thumb.*

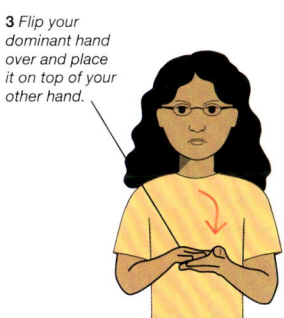

3 *Flip your dominant hand over and place it on top of your other hand.*

What

1 *Hold your arms out to your sides, with the palms facing up and fingers spread out.*

2 *Shake your hands lightly from side to side.*

TIP

Questioning words, including "what" and "why," should be signed with furrowed eyebrows.

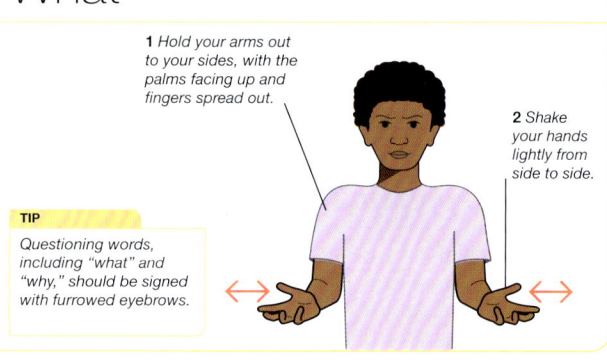

Who

1 *Make a fist with your dominant hand. Point upward with your index finger and touch the thumb to your chin.*

2 *Bend your index finger up and down a few times.*

The thumb does not move.

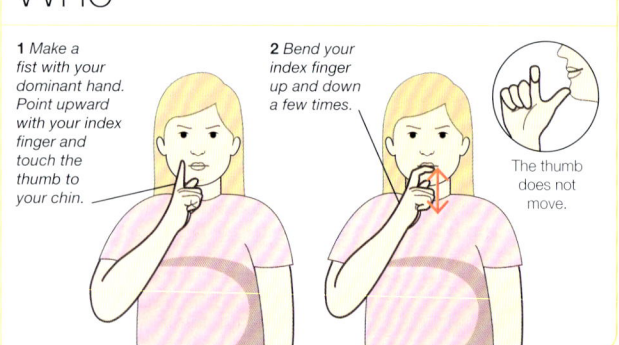

When

Left hand
dominant

1 *Curl both hands into fists, with the index fingers extended.*

2 *Move your dominant hand toward your other hand, but hold it higher.*

3 *Make a circle with your dominant index finger around the other index finger, then touch their fingertips.*

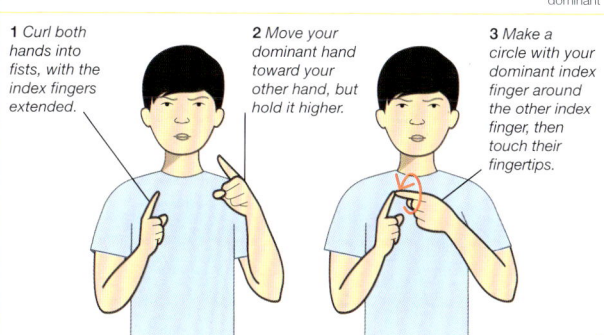

Why

1 *Bend the middle finger of your dominant hand and place it near your head.*

2 *Wriggle your middle finger up and down a few times.*

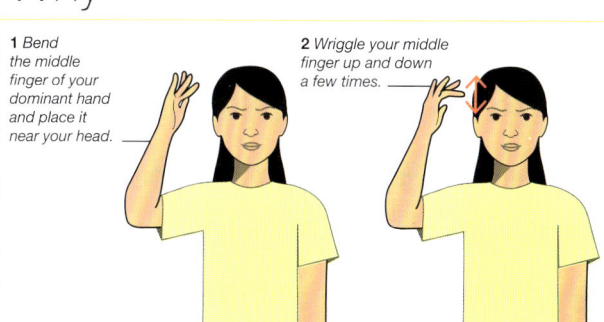

Which

Furrowing your eyebrows turns "which" into "which?" This sign is used with other signs to ask questions like "which one?" or "which color?"

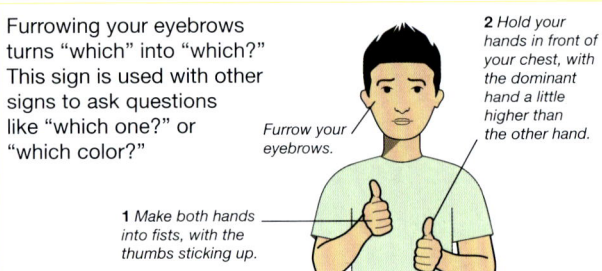

Furrow your eyebrows.

1 *Make both hands into fists, with the thumbs sticking up.*

2 *Hold your hands in front of your chest, with the dominant hand a little higher than the other hand.*

How

Left hand dominant

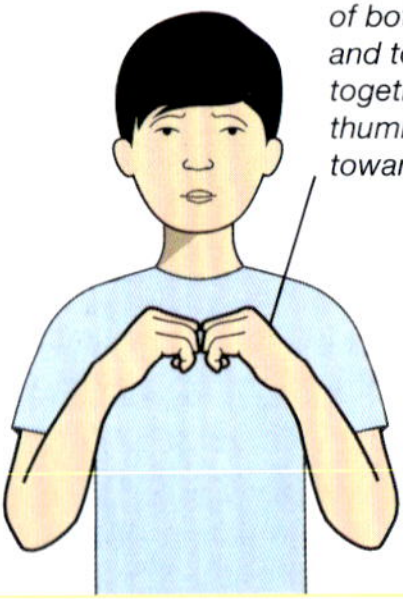

1 *Curl the fingers of both of your hands and touch the knuckles together, with the thumbs pointing toward your chest.*

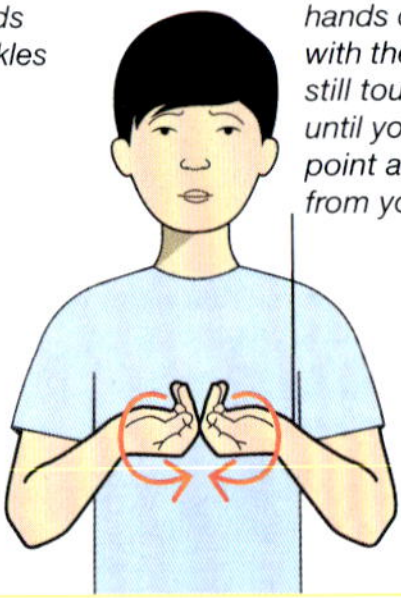

2 *Turn both hands outward, with the knuckles still touching, until your thumbs point away from you.*

3 Move both hands up and down a few times, in turn, so that one hand is always higher than the other.

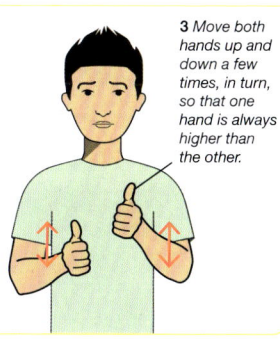

Where

Furrow your eyebrows.

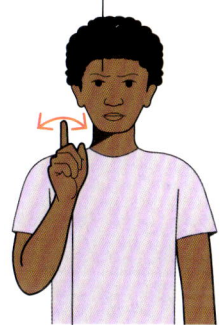

Curl your dominant hand into a fist, facing outward, with the index finger pointing up. Then waggle the wrist from side to side.

TIP

Move your hand from the wrist instead of wiggling your finger when signing this word.

There

1 Relax your dominant hand at shoulder height, with the palm facing up.

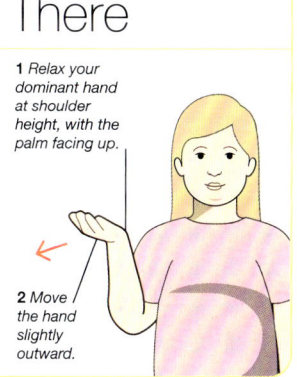

2 Move the hand slightly outward.

How are you?

Raising our eyebrows or bringing them together in a frown can turn a single word or sentence in ASL into a question.

Furrow your eyebrows as if you're asking a question.

Tilt your head slightly forward.

1 *Slightly curl both your hands and touch your knuckles together in front of your chest, with the thumbs toward you.*

How

Fine

The word "fine" can mean several things. This sign is used when describing how good something is or how we are feeling, not for a fee or when something is thin.

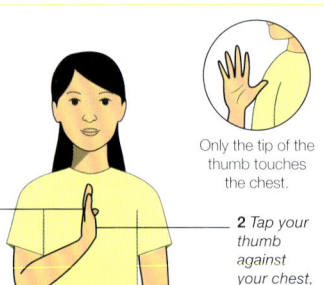

Only the tip of the thumb touches the chest.

1 *Turn the palm of your dominant hand toward your nondominant side. Spread its fingers loosely and point your thumb at your chest.*

2 *Tap your thumb against your chest, twice.*

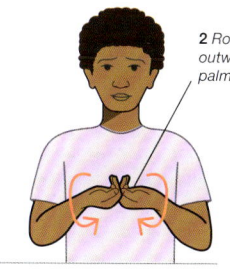

2 *Rotate your wrists outward until your palms face upward.*

3 *Point the index finger of your dominant hand at the person you are talking to.*

You

So-so

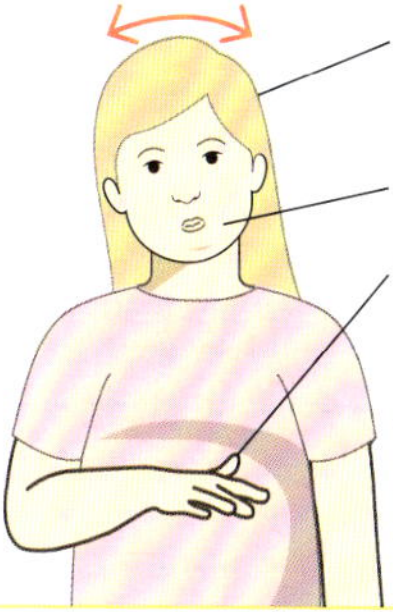

Shake your head slightly from side to side.

Pucker your lips.

1 *Hold your hand in front of your chest, with your palm facing down and the fingers spread slightly apart.*

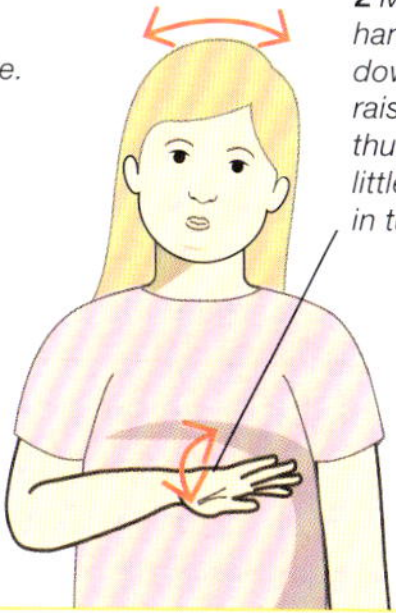

2 *Move your hand up and down lightly, raising the thumb and little finger in turn.*

Hello

1 Raise your dominant hand to the side of your head. Hold it flat, with the palm facing out and the thumb tucked in.

2 Tilt your hand to the dominant side then move it away from your head.

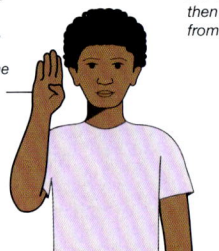
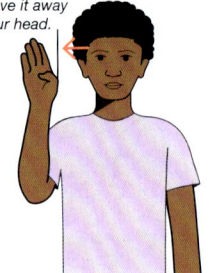

What is your name?

To ask someone their name, sign the words "what," "your," and "name." Furrow your eyebrows to make it clear that you are asking a question.

TIP

You can make this question shorter by signing just "name you?" or "your name?"

1 Move both your hands to your sides, with the fingers spread apart and palms facing up, then shake them lightly from side to side.

What

My name is...

To tell someone your name, sign the words "my" and "name," then fingerspell your name (see pages 156–157).

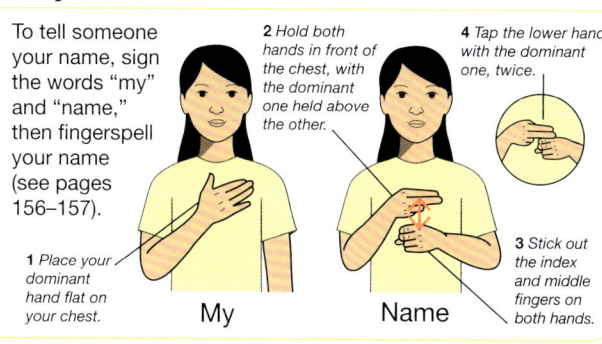

1 *Place your dominant hand flat on your chest.*

My

2 *Hold both hands in front of the chest, with the dominant one held above the other.*

4 *Tap the lower hand with the dominant one, twice.*

3 *Stick out the index and middle fingers on both hands.*

Name

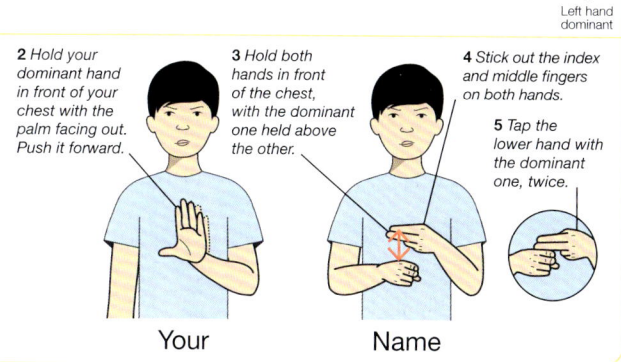

Left hand dominant

2 *Hold your dominant hand in front of your chest with the palm facing out. Push it forward.*

Your

3 *Hold both hands in front of the chest, with the dominant one held above the other.*

4 *Stick out the index and middle fingers on both hands.*

5 *Tap the lower hand with the dominant one, twice.*

Name

Nice to meet you.

This statement may be signed without using the word "to." It can be made even shorter by signing just "nice" and "meet" while leaning forward.

1 *Relax your nondominant hand and hold it in front of you, with its palm facing up.*

2 *Put your dominant hand on top of the other hand, with the palm facing down.*

Nice

4 *Raise your hands and point both index fingers upward, with the rest of your fingers curled into fists.*

5 *Move your hands toward each other.*

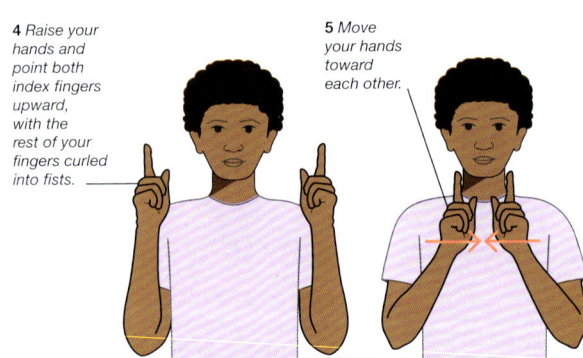

Meet

3 *Slide your dominant hand across your other hand, moving it away from you.*

Thank you

1 *Touch your chin with the fingers of your dominant hand.*

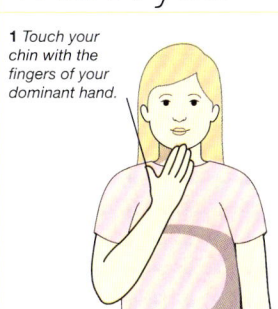

6 *Point the index finger of your dominant hand toward the person you are talking to.*

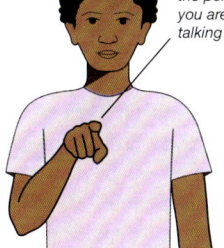

You

2 *Move your hand forward and downward, with the palm facing up.*

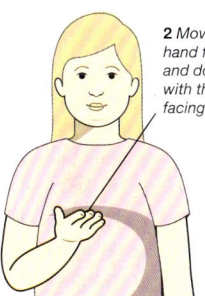

TIP

Use both hands when thanking a large group or showing someone that you are very thankful to them.

Are you deaf?

1 Make your dominant hand into a fist, with the index finger sticking out and touching your ear.

Raise your eyebrows, so it's clear that you're asking a question.

2 Lower your hand and touch the side of your mouth with the index finger.

3 Point your index finger at the person you're talking to.

Deaf

You

What is the sign for...?

If you don't know the sign for something, you can ask about it by pointing to the object or fingerspelling the word for it, before using the signs shown here.

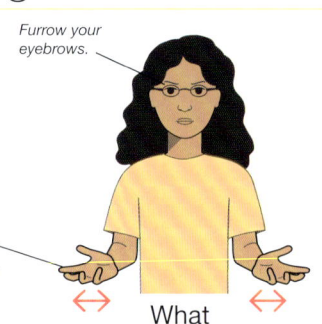

Furrow your eyebrows.

1 Open your hands and move them from side to side in front of you, with the palms facing up.

What

I'm hearing.

This sign is used to explain that you can hear.

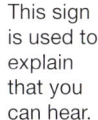

1 *Point the index finger of your dominant hand at your chest, with the other fingers curled into a fist.*

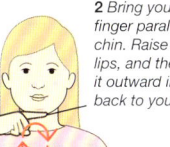

2 *Bring your index finger parallel to your chin. Raise it to your lips, and then move it outward in a circle back to your chin.*

I

Hearing

2 *Make both hands into fists, with the index fingers sticking out and facing up.*

3 *Make circles toward you with the index fingers of your hands, one after the other.*

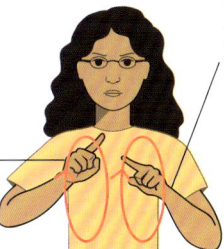

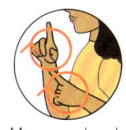

Move your hands in alternating circles like the tires of a bicycle.

Sign

What time is it?

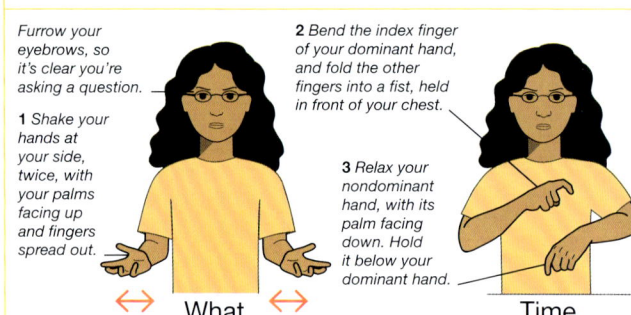

Furrow your eyebrows, so it's clear you're asking a question.

1 *Shake your hands at your side, twice, with your palms facing up and fingers spread out.*

2 *Bend the index finger of your dominant hand, and fold the other fingers into a fist, held in front of your chest.*

3 *Relax your nondominant hand, with its palm facing down. Hold it below your dominant hand.*

↔ What ↔

Time

It's 7:30.

To give the time, sign the number for the hour first, followed by the number of minutes past the hour.

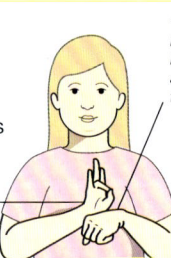

2 *Place your dominant hand on the other, palm facing out and slightly toward the nondominant side. Touch the ring finger to the thumb.*

1 *Make your nondominant hand into a fist, and hold it in front of your belly.*

3 *Move your dominant hand up in front of your face.*

7 o'clock

4 *Tap the index finger of your dominant hand against the wrist of your nondominant hand, twice.*

5 *Make both hands into fists in front of your chest, with the palms facing up and the thumbs and little fingers sticking out.*

6 *Move your hands down in front of your belly.*

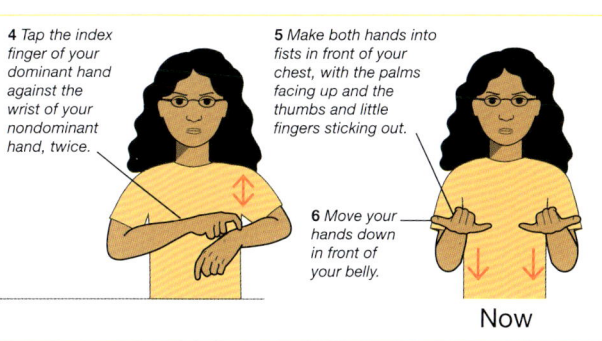

Now

4 *Curl in the ring and little fingers of your dominant hand, keeping the other fingers extended.*

5 *Make a zero with your dominant hand by curling your fingers and touching your thumb to your index and middle fingers.*

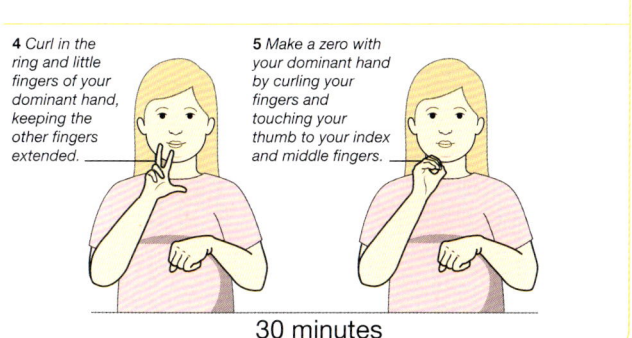

30 minutes

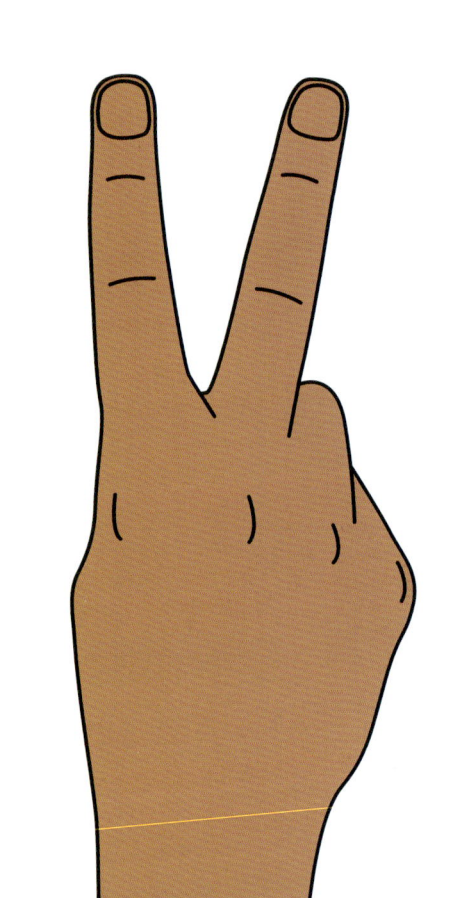

Chapter 2

HOME AND FAMILY

Here are the signs for the people, animals, and things in your home—including your pets! You can also learn how to ask for directions or invite people over to your home. Discover how to form different sentences using these signs.

◀ ASL sign for number 2

Mom

Touch the thumb of your dominant hand to your chin, with the palm facing your nondominant side.

TIP

All female signs are made on the lower part of the face, around the chin.

Keep your fingers spread apart and the palm flat.

Grandpa

Left hand dominant

1 *Touch the thumb of your dominant hand to the side of your forehead, with the palm facing your nondominant side.*

2 *Move your hand forward, making a pair of dips.*

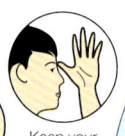

Keep your fingers spread apart and the palm flat.

Make two small curves.

Dad

Touch the thumb of your dominant hand to the side of your forehead, with the palm facing your nondominant side.

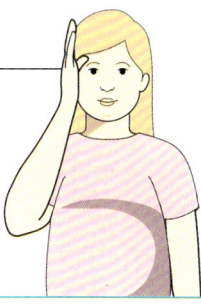

TIP

All male signs are made on the upper part of the face, around the forehead.

Keep your fingers spread apart and the palm flat.

Grandma

1 *Touch the thumb of your dominant hand to your chin, with your palm facing the nondominant side.*

Keep your fingers spread apart and the palm flat.

2 *Move your hand forward, making a pair of dips.*

Make two small curves.

Sister

1 Make both your hands into fists, and touch your chin with your dominant hand.

2 Hold your nondominant hand in front of you.

3 Move your dominant hand downward, with its index finger sticking out.

4 Stick out the index finger of your other hand and point it away from you.

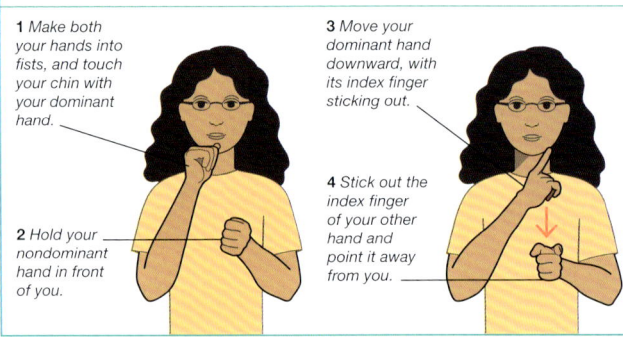

Brother

1 Curl both your hands into fists, and touch your forehead with your dominant hand.

2 Hold your nondominant hand in front of you.

3 Move your dominant hand downward, with its index finger sticking out.

4 Point the index finger of your other hand outward.

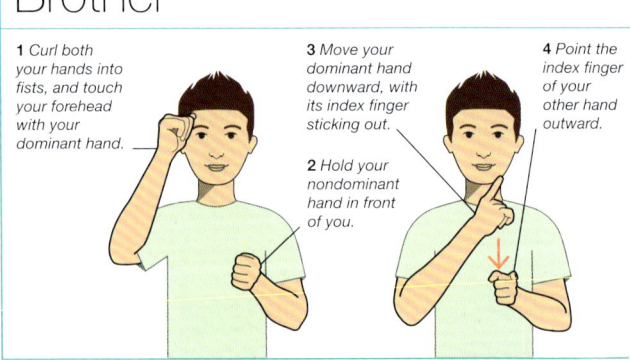

5 *Stack your dominant hand on top of your other hand.*

Aunt

Left hand dominant

Make your dominant hand into a fist near the lower half of your face. Move it up and down slightly, twice.

5 *Stack your dominant hand on top of your other hand.*

Uncle

1 *Hold your dominant hand in a fist at the side of your head, facing forward. Stick up the index and middle fingers.*

2 *Move your arm up and down slightly, twice.*

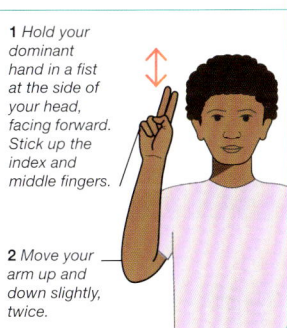

Pet

2 *Relax your dominant hand and place it on top of the nondominant fist, with the palm facing down.*

3 *Raise your dominant hand, bend the fingers slightly, and then pat your nondominant fist, twice.*

1 *Make a fist with your nondominant hand, with the palm facing down.*

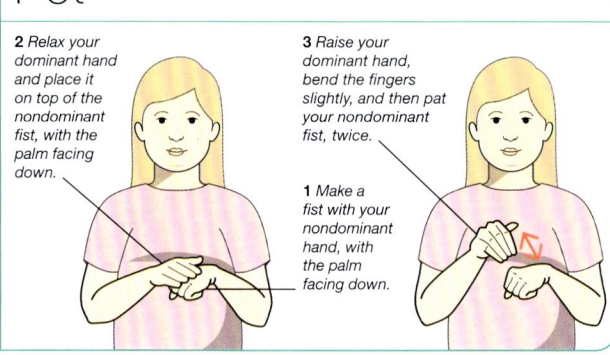

Dog

1 *Touch the middle finger of your dominant hand to your thumb, then stick out the index finger and fold in all other fingers.*

2 *Snap your middle finger and thumb, twice, then bring your thumb near your index finger and fold in all other fingers.*

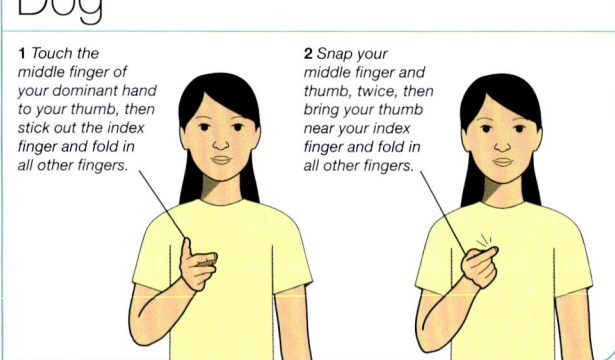

Cat

1 *Spread the fingers of both your hands, bringing the thumbs and index fingers near your mouth.*

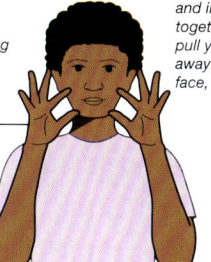

2 *Pinch the thumbs and index fingers together, and pull your hands away from your face, twice.*

Bird

1 *Bring your dominant hand near your mouth, and make a fist while sticking out your thumb and index finger.*

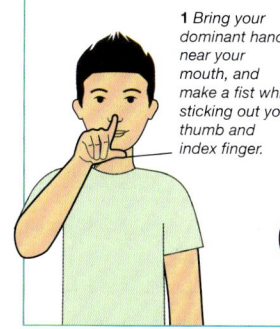

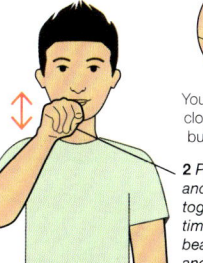

Your hand should be close to your mouth but not touching it.

2 *Pinch your thumb and index finger together several times, like a bird's beak opening and closing.*

Bedroom

The ASL sign for "bedroom" combines the signs for the words "bed" and "room."

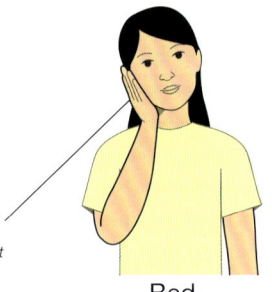

1 *Tilt your head into the palm of your dominant hand, kept against your cheek.*

Bed

Window

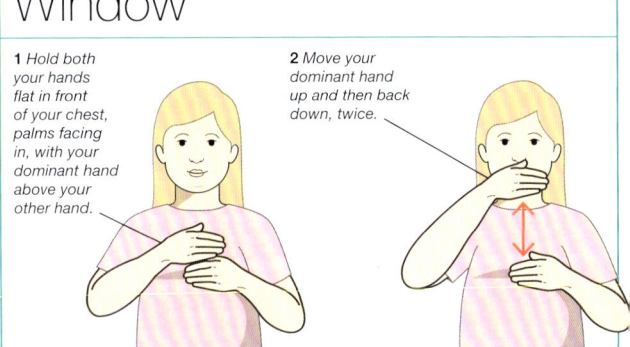

1 *Hold both your hands flat in front of your chest, palms facing in, with your dominant hand above your other hand.*

2 *Move your dominant hand up and then back down, twice.*

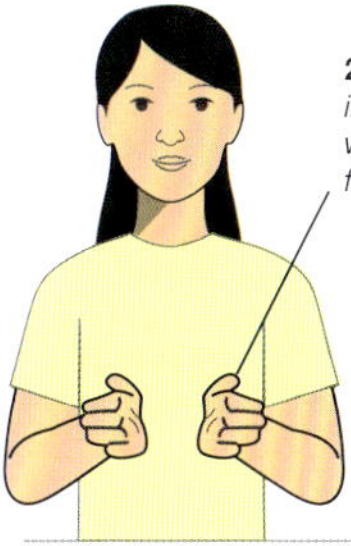

2 *Bring both hands in front of your chest with the palms flat and facing each other.*

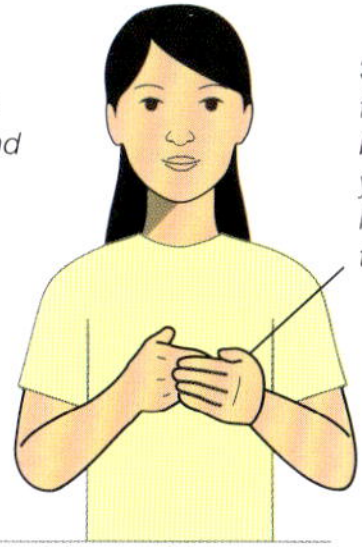

3 *Fold your fingers inward, with your dominant hand behind the other.*

Room

Door

Left hand dominant

1 *Hold your hands flat in front of your mouth, with the palms facing forward and the thumb sides touching.*

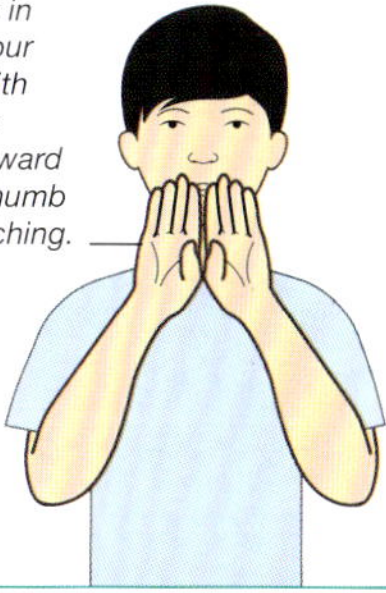

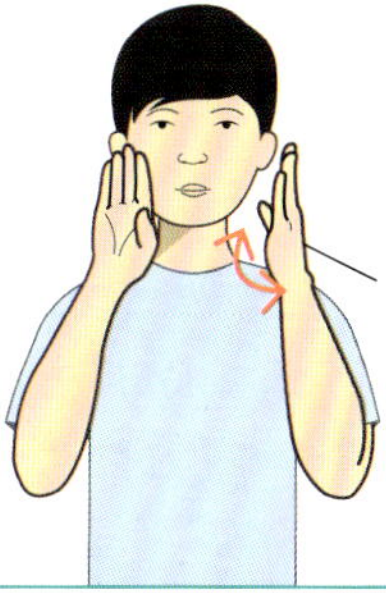

2 *Turn your dominant hand sideways, palm facing the other hand, then bring it back to how you started. Do this twice.*

TV

Left hand dominant

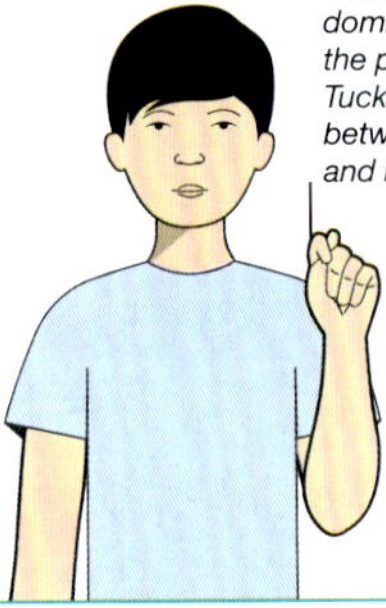

1 *Make a fist with your dominant hand, with the palm facing out. Tuck your thumb up between your middle and index fingers.*

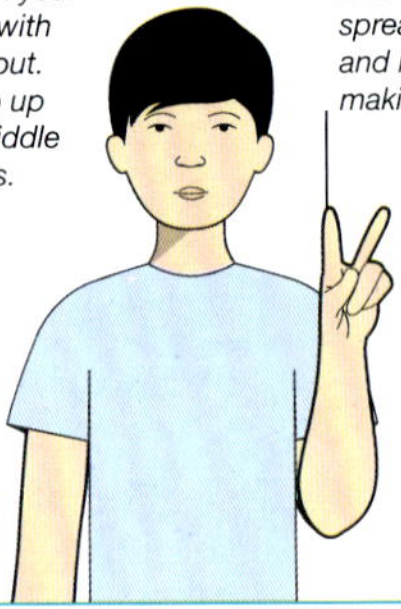

2 *Stick out and spread your index and middle fingers, making a "V" shape.*

Computer

2 *Make a "C" shape with your dominant hand above your nondominant arm.*

3 *Slide the curled dominant hand over the lower arm, slightly toward the elbow, then back to the wrist, twice.*

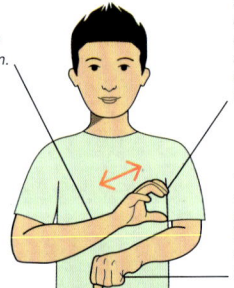

TIP

Keep your fingers together in the curl so that the "C" shape is clear.

1 *Make a fist with your nondominant hand in front of you, with the palm facing down.*

Phone

1 *Make a fist with your dominant hand but stick out your thumb and little finger. Hold your hand near your cheek.*

2 *Tap your curled fingers against your cheek, twice.*

Tablet

2 *Keep your dominant hand relaxed, but bend your middle finger so that it touches the palm of your other hand.*

3 *Drag the middle finger of your dominant hand back and forth across the other palm, twice.*

1 *Hold your nondominant hand loosely in front of you, with the palm facing up.*

Slide your middle finger across the palm of your other hand as if you are scrolling through content on a tablet.

You come to my house.

There is no need to sign the word "to" when it is implied by another word in the sentence. Here, "to" is implied as part of the verb "come," so you can skip it.

1 *Make a fist with your dominant hand and point the index finger at the person you are talking to.*

You

4 *Place your dominant hand flat on your chest.*

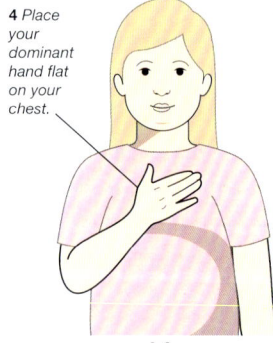

My

5 *Make a slanting roof with your hands slightly bent and your fingers straight and pointing up. Touch the tips of your fingers.*

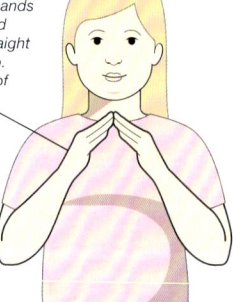

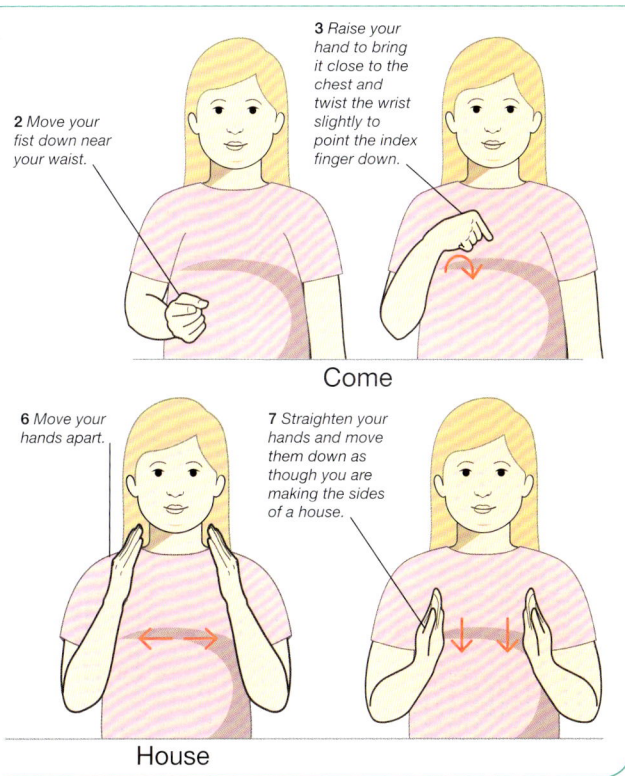

2 *Move your fist down near your waist.*

3 *Raise your hand to bring it close to the chest and twist the wrist slightly to point the index finger down.*

Come

6 *Move your hands apart.*

7 *Straighten your hands and move them down as though you are making the sides of a house.*

House

How do I get there?

When you want to get to a place, you can use this sequence of signs to ask for directions.

Furrow your eyebrows as if you're asking a question.

1 *Slightly curl both your hands and touch your knuckles together in front of your chest, with the thumbs toward you.*

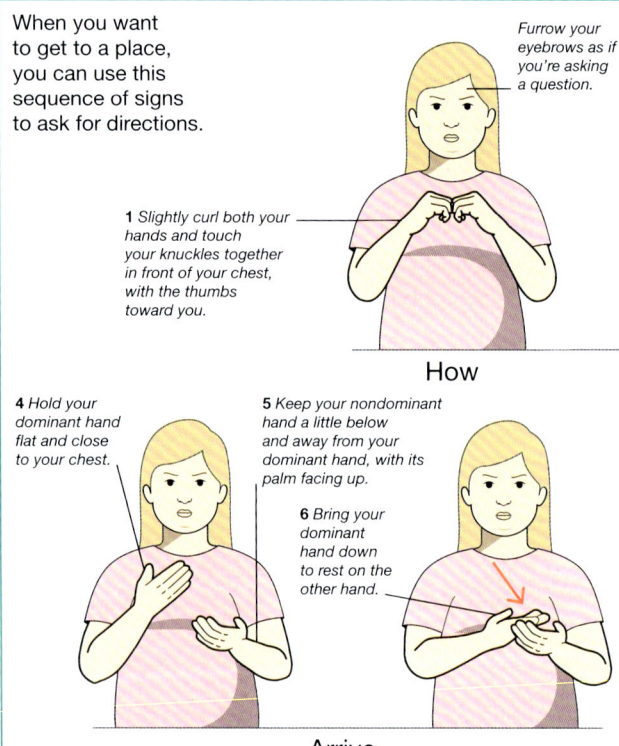

How

4 *Hold your dominant hand flat and close to your chest.*

5 *Keep your nondominant hand a little below and away from your dominant hand, with its palm facing up.*

6 *Bring your dominant hand down to rest on the other hand.*

Arrive

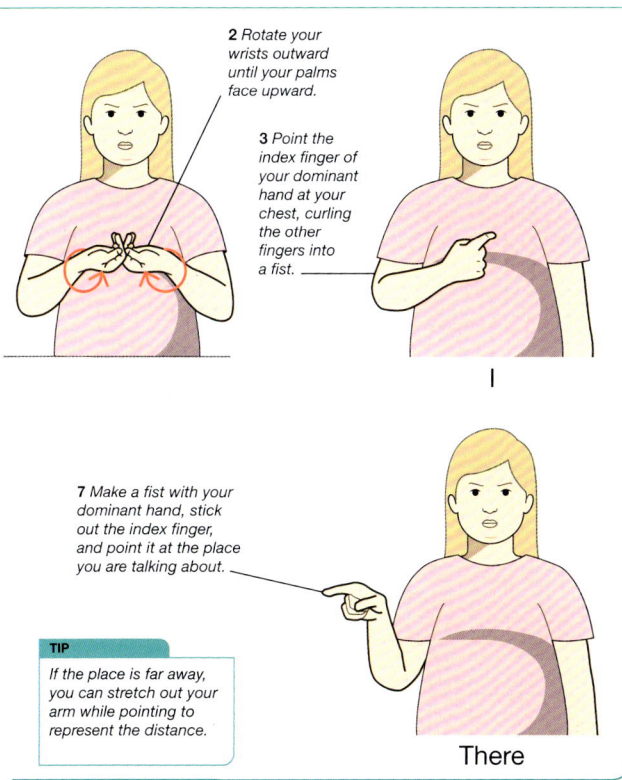

2 Rotate your wrists outward until your palms face upward.

3 Point the index finger of your dominant hand at your chest, curling the other fingers into a fist.

I

7 Make a fist with your dominant hand, stick out the index finger, and point it at the place you are talking about.

TIP

If the place is far away, you can stretch out your arm while pointing to represent the distance.

There

Can I go to the bathroom, please?

Signing "please" after "bathroom," with raised eyebrows means "Can I go to the bathroom, please?" but signing just "bathroom" with that expression makes it "Do you need to go to the bathroom?"

TIP

You can also sign "bathroom" by twisting your fist rather than moving it sideways.

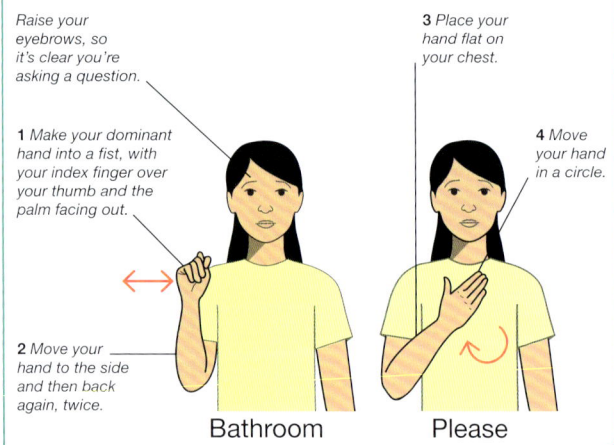

Raise your eyebrows, so it's clear you're asking a question.

1 *Make your dominant hand into a fist, with your index finger over your thumb and the palm facing out.*

2 *Move your hand to the side and then back again, twice.*

3 *Place your hand flat on your chest.*

4 *Move your hand in a circle.*

Bathroom

Please

Close the window.

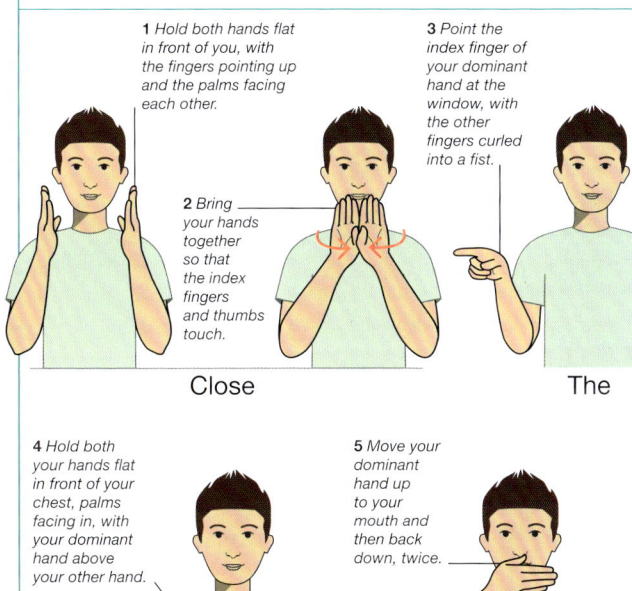

1 *Hold both hands flat in front of you, with the fingers pointing up and the palms facing each other.*

2 *Bring your hands together so that the index fingers and thumbs touch.*

3 *Point the index finger of your dominant hand at the window, with the other fingers curled into a fist.*

Close

The

4 *Hold both your hands flat in front of your chest, palms facing in, with your dominant hand above your other hand.*

5 *Move your dominant hand up to your mouth and then back down, twice.*

Window

Where is the kitchen?

2 *Hold your dominant hand above your other hand. Point your index finger up and middle finger to your nondominant side. Curl in the other fingers, with the thumb touching your middle finger.*

Furrow your eyebrows in a questioning expression.

1 *Keep your nondominant hand relaxed in front of you, with the palm facing up.*

TIP

You can also sign "kitchen" by fingerspelling "K" and shaking your wrist from side to side.

Kitchen

It's through there.

Make a fist with your dominant hand, stick out the index finger, and point it in the direction of the place you are talking about.

TIP

You can squint your eyes to indicate that the place you are pointing at is a bit distant.

There

3 *Tap your nondominant hand with your dominant one. Flip the dominant hand and place it on the other palm, with its curled fingers facing you.*

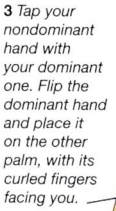 

4 *Hold the hand in a fist in front of you, facing away from you, with the index finger sticking out.*

5 *Shake your wrist from side to side.*

Where

I don't know.

Shake your head and look unsure.

1 *Bend your dominant hand in half, with the fingers held together, and touch the side of your forehead with it.*

2 *Turn your hand so that its palm faces forward, while moving it away from you.*

Don't know

Chapter 3

FEELINGS

Using your face to express yourself is important in ASL. This is particularly true when it comes to signs about your feelings. "Happy" must be signed with a smile, and "sad" with an upset expression. Most feelings have their own unique sign, but a few similar emotions share one.

◀ ASL sign for number 3

Feel

1 Hold your dominant hand in front of your chest and spread the fingers, with the middle finger bent inward.

2 Move your hand upward, with the middle finger lightly brushing against your chest.

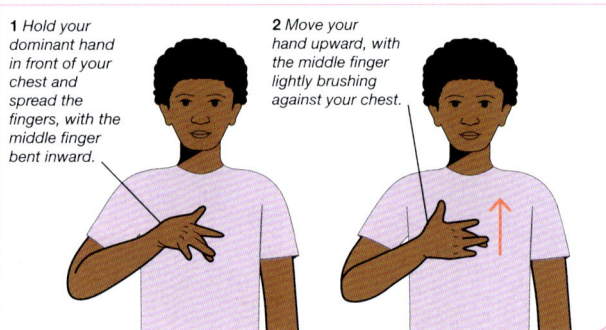

Sad

1 Hold both hands at the sides of your face, with the palms facing in and fingers spread apart.

2 Tilt your head slightly

Have a sad expression on your face.

3 Pull both your hands downward.

TIP

The head tilt should just be a small movement, not a full nod or shake.

Happy

1 Place the palm of your dominant hand on your chest, with the thumb sticking out.

Be bright-eyed and have a smile on your face.

2 Brush your hand lightly up your chest, twice.

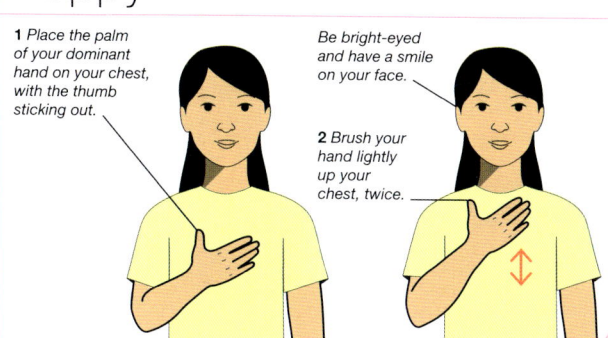

Scared

🖐 Left hand dominant

1 Make both hands into fists and hold them in front of your chest, with the palms facing in.

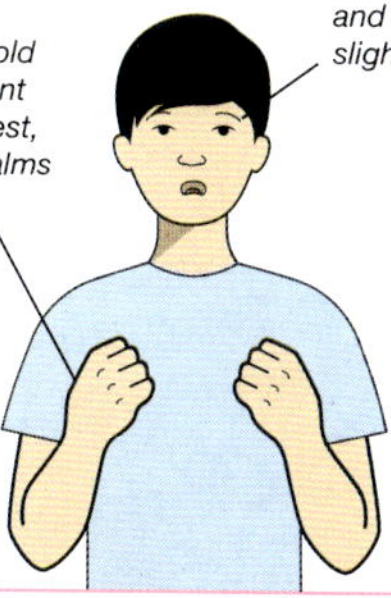

Raise your eyebrows, and open your mouth slightly to look scared.

3 Lift your shoulders.

2 Flare out your fingers and move your hands toward each other, keeping the dominant hand above the other.

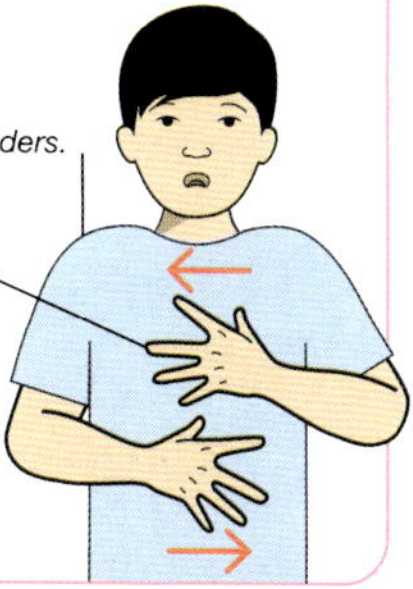

Jealous

1 *Make your dominant hand into a fist. Stick out your index finger, bend it slightly, and touch it to the corner of your mouth.*

2 *Twist your hand so that the palm faces you.*

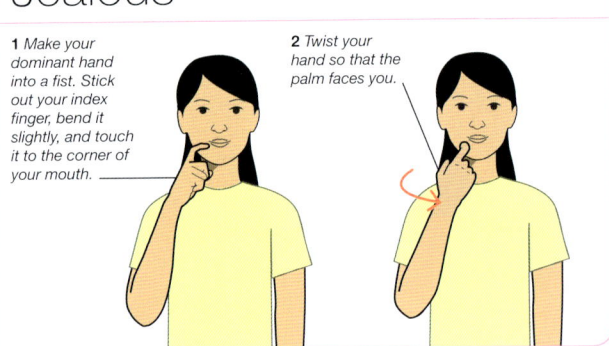

Surprised

1 *Curl both hands into fists near your eyes, with the thumbs and index fingers touching together.*

2 *Stick out the thumbs and index fingers of both your hands. Point the index fingers upward.*

Lift your eyebrows and widen your eyes.

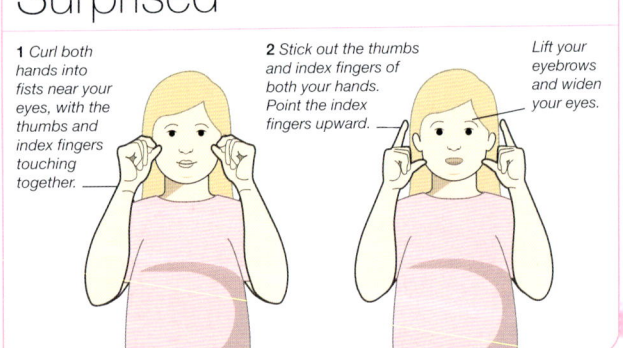

Angry

Furrow your eyebrows to show that you are angry.

1 *Hold your dominant hand in front of your face, with the palm facing in and fingers spread out.*

2 *Curl it into a claw in front of your chin.*

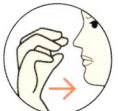

Move your hand slightly toward your mouth as it forms a claw.

TIP

When you repeat the "clawing" movement a few times, you make the sign for "grumpy."

Bored

Lower your eyebrows.

1 *Curl your dominant hand into a fist, stick out your index finger, and touch it to the side of your nose.*

2 *Turn your hand around so that it faces you.*

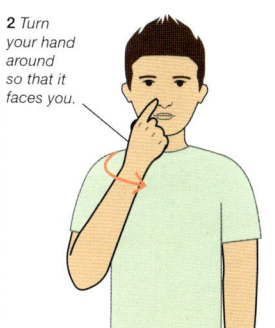

Excited

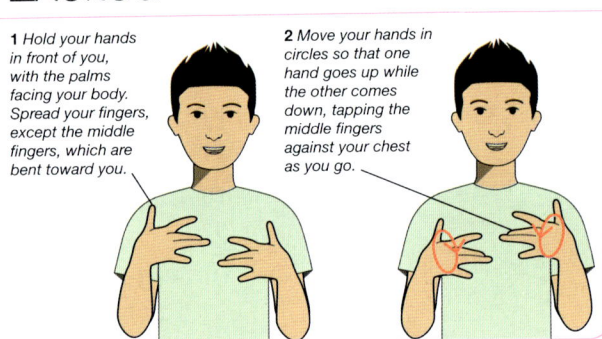

1 Hold your hands in front of you, with the palms facing your body. Spread your fingers, except the middle fingers, which are bent toward you.

2 Move your hands in circles so that one hand goes up while the other comes down, tapping the middle fingers against your chest as you go.

Curious

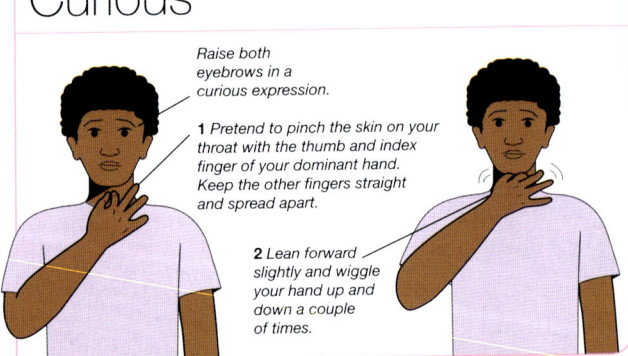

Raise both eyebrows in a curious expression.

1 Pretend to pinch the skin on your throat with the thumb and index finger of your dominant hand. Keep the other fingers straight and spread apart.

2 Lean forward slightly and wiggle your hand up and down a couple of times.

Love

Make fists with your hands and cross your arms against your chest, a bit like giving yourself a hug.

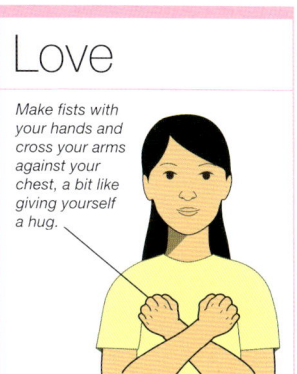

Proud

1 *Make a fist with your dominant hand but leave the thumb sticking out.*

2 *Point the thumb at yourself and move your hand up your chest.*

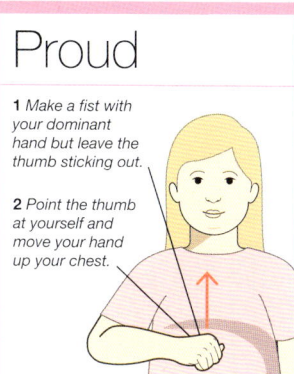

Embarrassed

1 *Place your hands on the sides of your face, with the palms facing in and the fingers spread out.*

Lower your eyebrows slightly to show embarrassment.

2 *Make circles with each hand in turn so that one hand goes up while the other moves down.*

Frustrated

1 *Hold your dominant hand in front of your chin, with the palm and fingers flat and facing away from you.*

Frown slightly to show you are frustrated.

2 *Make a circle toward your chin, tapping it with your fingers, twice.*

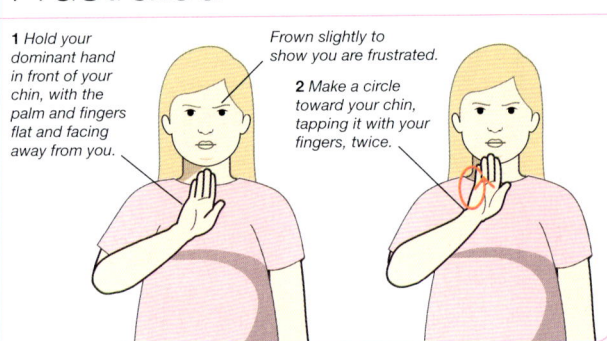

Nervous

Left hand dominant

1 *Hold both your hands in front of your chest, with the palms facing down and fingers spread apart. Shake them from the wrists.*

Furrow your eyebrows slightly to look nervous.

TIP

Shaking your hands this way, while moving them slightly away from your body, gives the sign for "anxious."

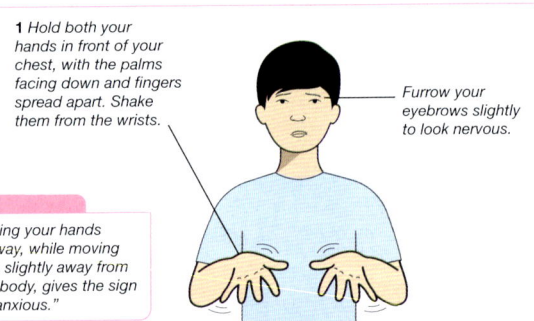

Disgusted

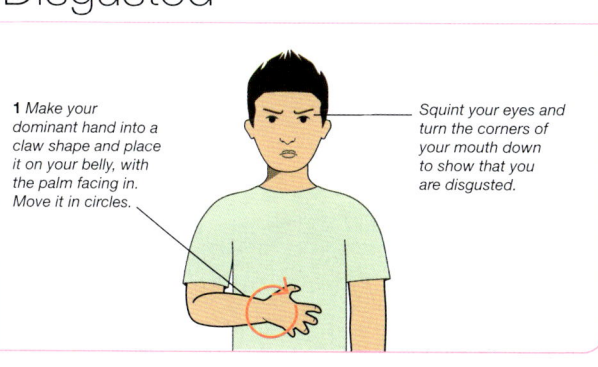

1 *Make your dominant hand into a claw shape and place it on your belly, with the palm facing in. Move it in circles.*

Squint your eyes and turn the corners of your mouth down to show that you are disgusted.

Tired

Drooping eyebrows

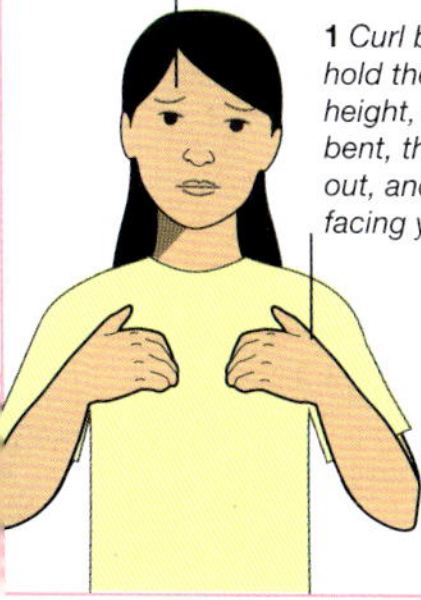

1 *Curl both hands and hold them at chest height, with wrists bent, thumbs sticking out, and the palms facing your body.*

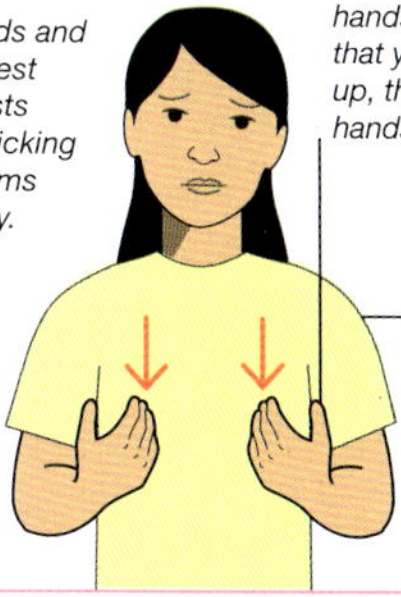

2 *Turn both your hands slightly so that your palms face up, then move your hands downward.*

3 *Slump your shoulders down at the same time.*

Hot

1 *Curl your dominant hand into a claw shape and hold it in front of your mouth.*

2 *Move the hand away from your mouth and turn it outward. Open your mouth at the same time.*

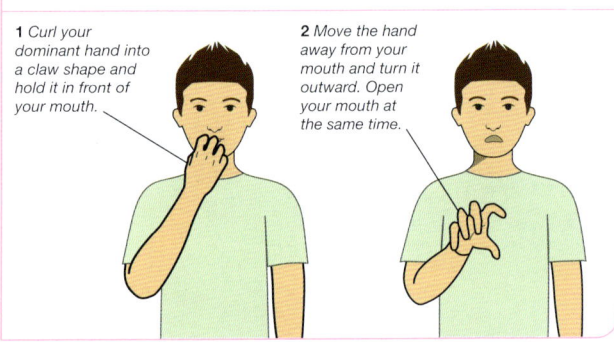

Cold

Curl both hands into fists and hold them in front of your chest, facing each other. Shake them as though you are shivering.

Narrow your eyes, purse your lips, and hunch up your shoulders as though you are cold.

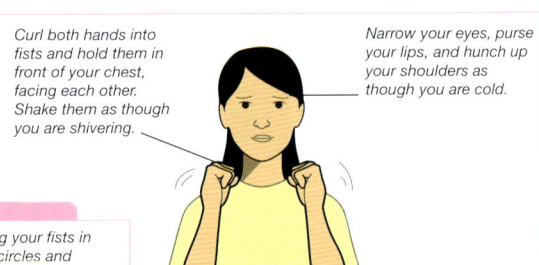

TIP

Moving your fists in small circles and mouthing the word "win" turns this into the sign for "winter."

Hurt

1 Fold your hands into fists and hold them in front of you. Point your index fingers at each other.

Make your face look like you are going to cry.

2 Move your hands toward each other and then away several times.

Safe

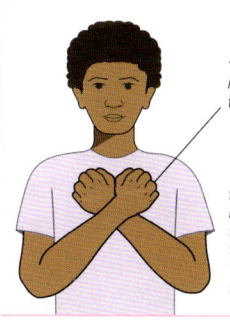

1 Close your hands into fists and cross them on your chest.

2 Move your hands away from the chest and to the sides, with the fists facing outward.

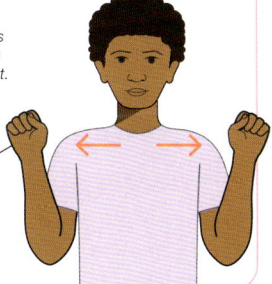

I'm nervous about the doctor's appointment.

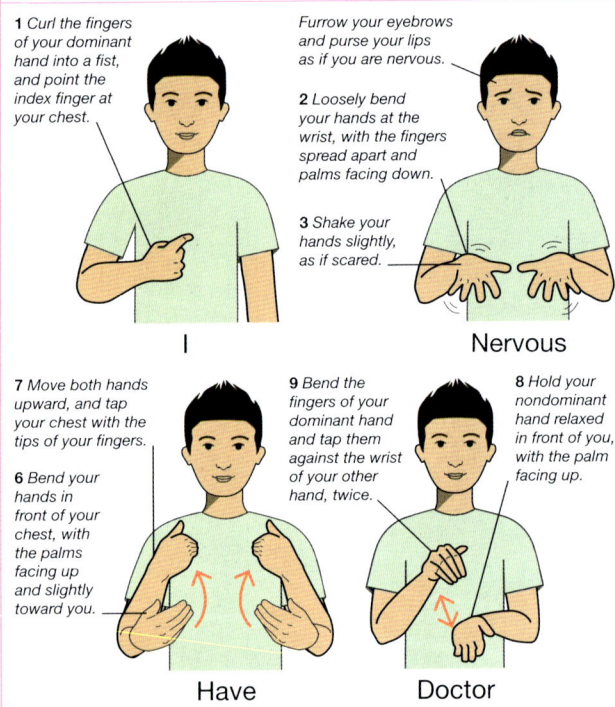

1 *Curl the fingers of your dominant hand into a fist, and point the index finger at your chest.*

Furrow your eyebrows and purse your lips as if you are nervous.

2 *Loosely bend your hands at the wrist, with the fingers spread apart and palms facing down.*

3 *Shake your hands slightly, as if scared.*

I

Nervous

7 *Move both hands upward, and tap your chest with the tips of your fingers.*

6 *Bend your hands in front of your chest, with the palms facing up and slightly toward you.*

9 *Bend the fingers of your dominant hand and tap them against the wrist of your other hand, twice.*

8 *Hold your nondominant hand relaxed in front of you, with the palm facing up.*

Have

Doctor

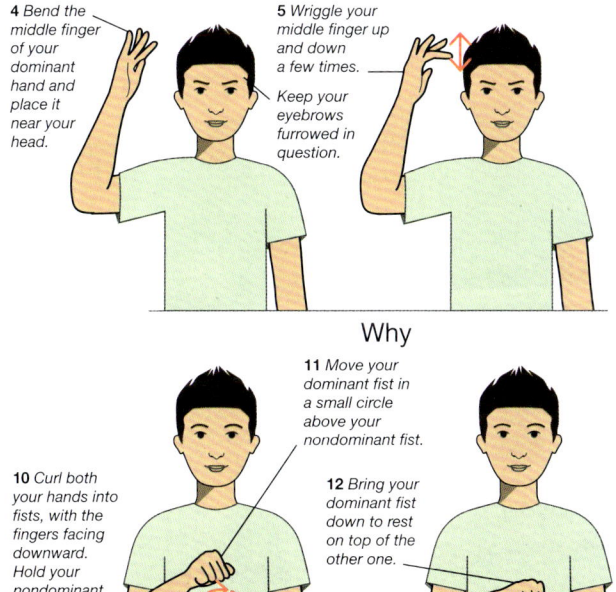

4 *Bend the middle finger of your dominant hand and place it near your head.*

5 *Wriggle your middle finger up and down a few times.*

Keep your eyebrows furrowed in question.

Why

10 *Curl both your hands into fists, with the fingers facing downward. Hold your nondominant hand in front of your belly.*

11 *Move your dominant fist in a small circle above your nondominant fist.*

12 *Bring your dominant fist down to rest on top of the other one.*

Appointment

You look excited.

1 Make a fist with your dominant hand in front of you and point your index finger at the person you are talking to.

2 Hold your dominant hand near your head. Curve it slightly, with the palm facing your nondominant side.

3 Twist your hand so the palm faces you.

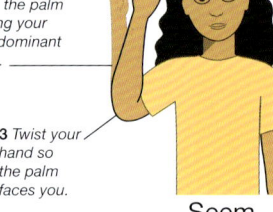

You

Seem

It's my birthday tomorrow.

1 Curl your dominant hand into a fist, with your thumb sticking out and touching your cheek.

2 Rotate the fist forward so that your thumb points up.

3 Place the hand flat on your chest.

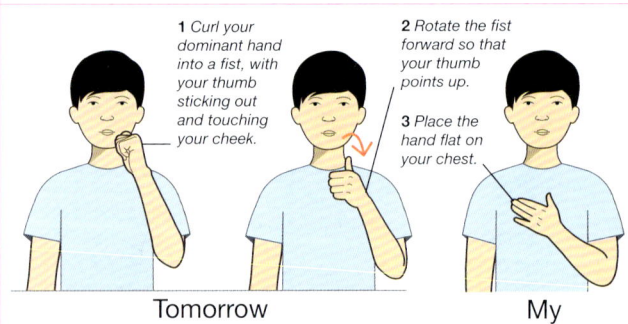

Tomorrow

My

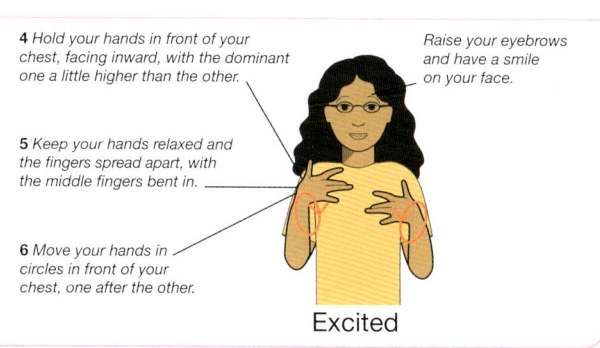

4 *Hold your hands in front of your chest, facing inward, with the dominant one a little higher than the other.*

Raise your eyebrows and have a smile on your face.

5 *Keep your hands relaxed and the fingers spread apart, with the middle fingers bent in.*

6 *Move your hands in circles in front of your chest, one after the other.*

Excited

Left hand dominant

5 *Lower the hand and touch your chest with your middle finger.*

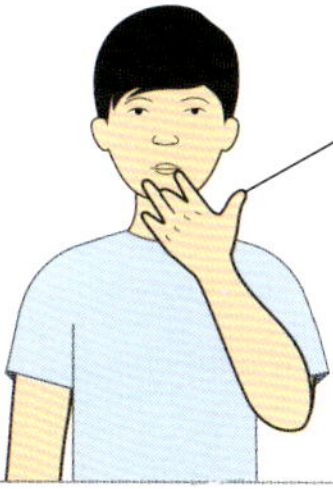

4 *Hold the hand near your face, with the fingers open and relaxed. Bend the middle finger and touch your chin.*

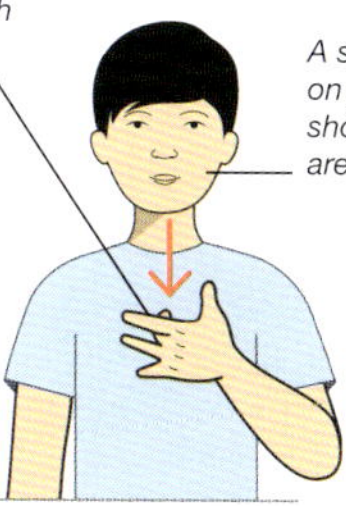

A slight smile on your face shows that you are happy.

Birthday

Do you like surprise parties?

1 *Make a fist with your dominant hand, but point the index finger at the person you are talking to.*

Raise your eyebrows, so it's clear you're asking a question.

TIP

You can also sign "party" by fingerspelling "P" with both hands and swinging them sideways.

You

4 *Make both hands into fists, with the index fingers touching the thumbs. Hold the fists near your eyes.*

Open your eyes and mouth wide, in surprise.

5 *Stick out the index finger and thumb on each hand.*

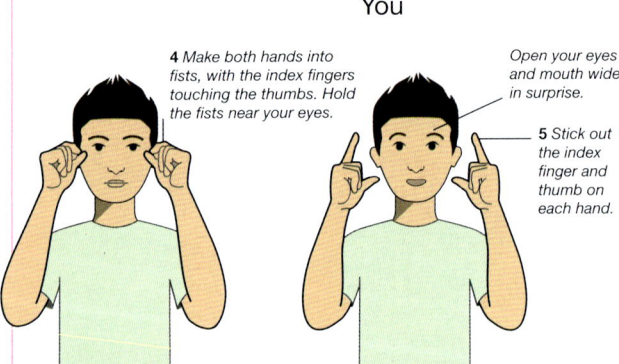

Surprise

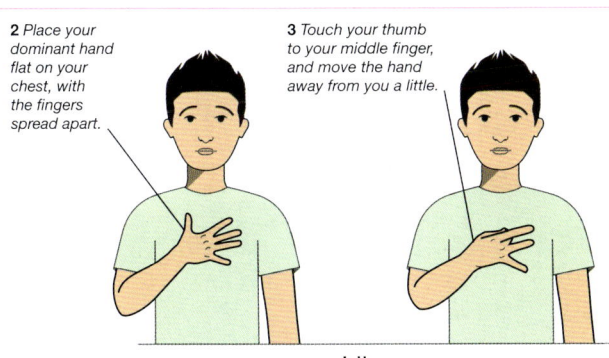

2 *Place your dominant hand flat on your chest, with the fingers spread apart.*

3 *Touch your thumb to your middle finger, and move the hand away from you a little.*

Like

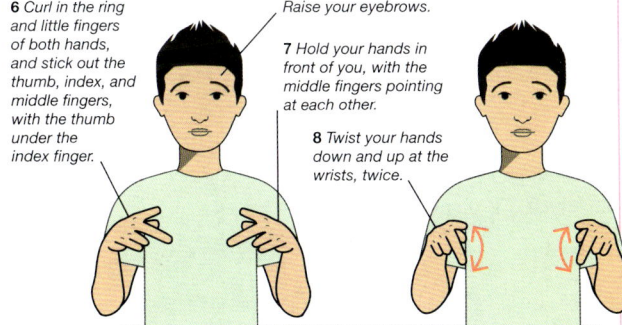

6 *Curl in the ring and little fingers of both hands, and stick out the thumb, index, and middle fingers, with the thumb under the index finger.*

Raise your eyebrows.

7 *Hold your hands in front of you, with the middle fingers pointing at each other.*

8 *Twist your hands down and up at the wrists, twice.*

Parties

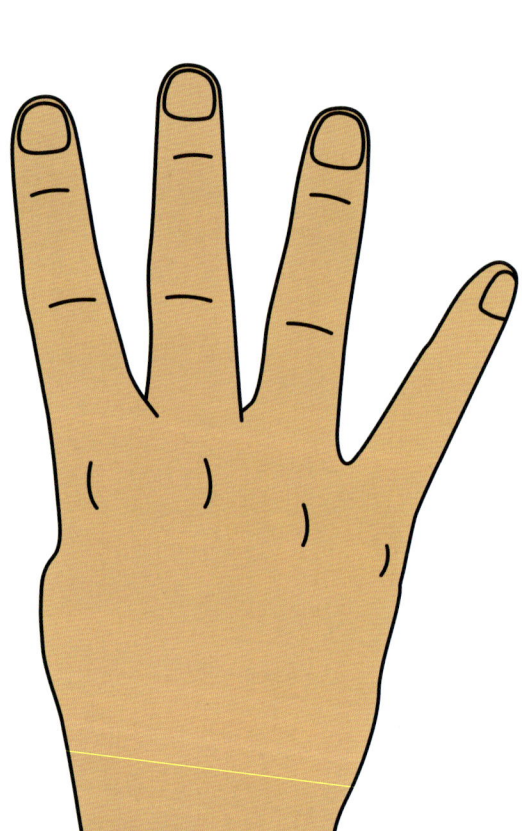

Chapter 4

FOOD AND DRINK

Many of us love to talk about food. Here are the signs for mealtimes, fruits, and everyday favorite meals such as sandwiches and pizza. Learn how to request food when you are hungry and ask for a glass of water when you are thirsty.

◀ ASL sign for number 4

Hungry

1 *Place your dominant hand on your chest and slightly curl your fingers.*

Have drooping eyelids and slightly turn down the corners of your mouth to show that you are hungry.

2 *Pull your hand down to your tummy.*

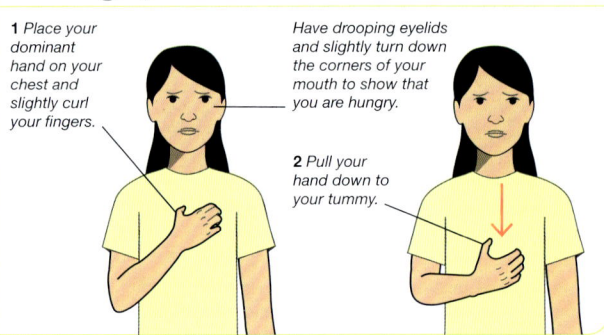

Thirsty

1 *Make a fist with your dominant hand, with the index finger pointing at the top of your throat.*

2 *Move your index finger to draw a line down your throat.*

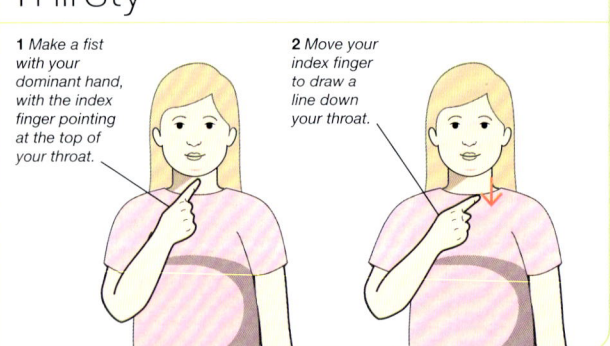

Full

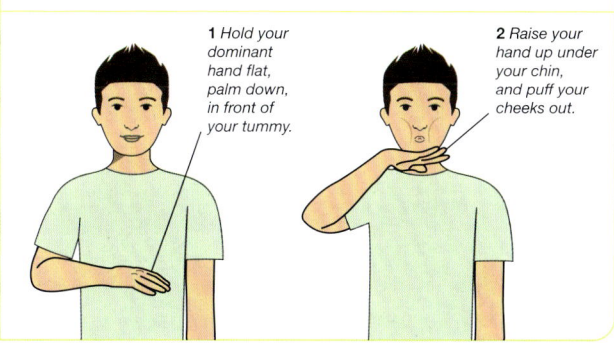

1 *Hold your dominant hand flat, palm down, in front of your tummy.*

2 *Raise your hand up under your chin, and puff your cheeks out.*

Eat

Left hand dominant

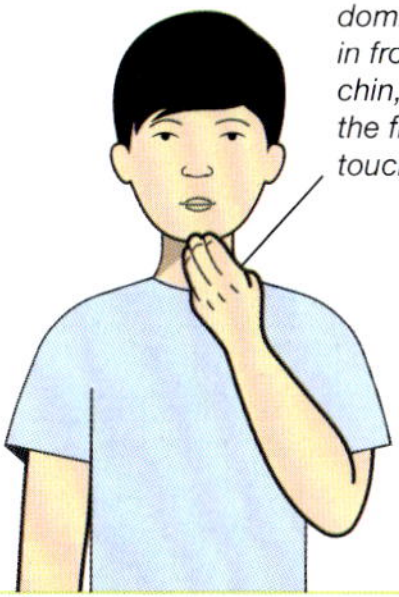

1 *Hold your dominant hand in front of your chin, with all the fingertips touching together.*

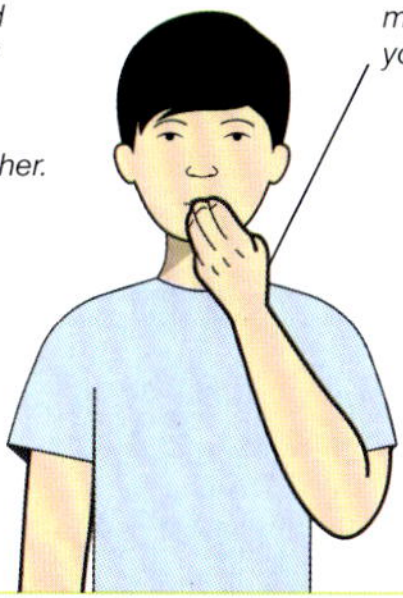

2 *Tap your mouth with your fingertips.*

Breakfast

1 *Hold your dominant hand flat near your mouth, with the thumb folded in.*

2 *Tap your chin with the tip of your index finger.*

Angle your palm away to the side and touch your index finger to your chin.

Drink

1 *Hold your dominant hand near your mouth. Loosely curl its fingers, with the thumb touching the bottom lip, as if you were holding a glass.*

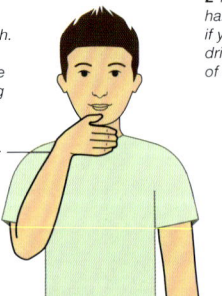

2 *Tilt your hand as if you were drinking out of a glass.*

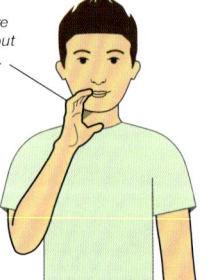

Dinner

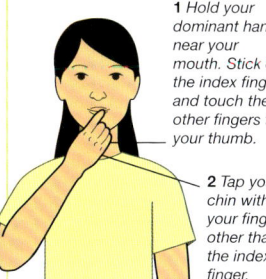

1 *Hold your dominant hand near your mouth. Stick out the index finger and touch the other fingers to your thumb.*

2 *Tap your chin with all your fingers other than the index finger.*

Lunch

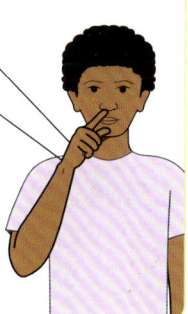

2 *Tap your chin with your thumb.*

1 *Make a fist with your dominant hand near your mouth, while sticking out your index finger and thumb.*

Water

Left hand dominant

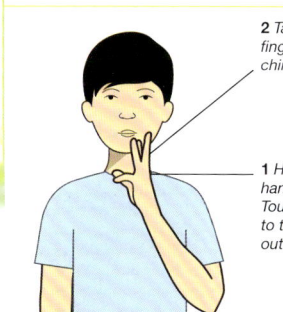

2 *Tap your index finger on your chin, twice.*

1 *Hold your dominant hand near your mouth. Touch the little finger to the thumb and stick out the other fingers.*

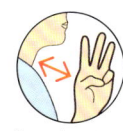

Spread apart your index, middle, and ring fingers in a "W" shape.

Ice cream

Left hand
dominant

1 *Curl the fingers of your dominant hand into a fist in front of your chin.*

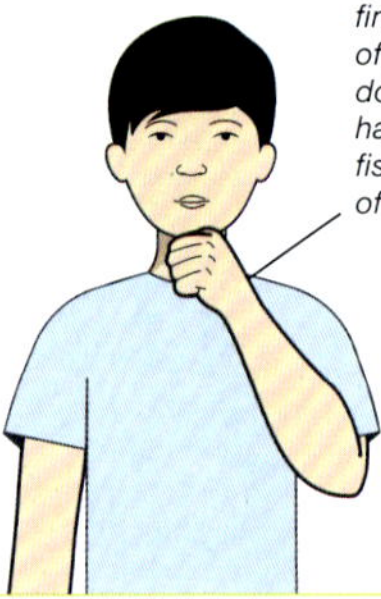

2 *Move the fist in a circle in front of your chin, twice.*

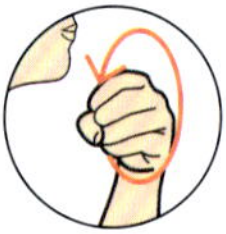

The fist moves up, in, down, and away from you, twice.

Cereal

1 Curl your dominant hand into a fist, with the index finger sticking out. Hold this finger near the corner of your mouth, with the fist facing down.

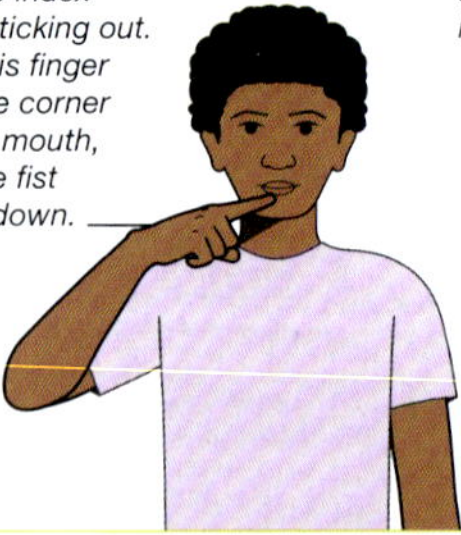

2 *Move the hand across your mouth while bending and then sticking out your index finger a few times.*

The index finger is extended straight when sticking it out.

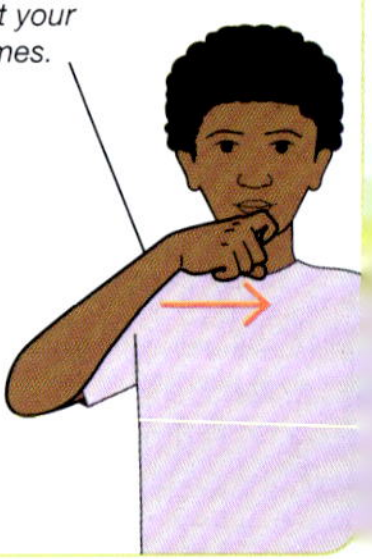

Cookie

2 *Place the fingers of your dominant hand in a claw shape on your other palm.*

3 *Lift your claw, twist it to the right, and then lower it back down onto the other palm.*

1 *Hold your nondominant hand flat in front of you, tilted slightly toward your dominant side.*

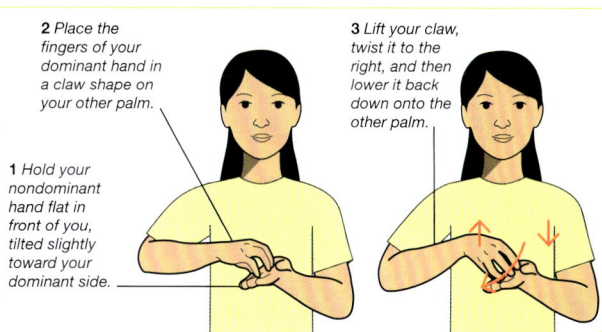

Cheese

1 *Hold your dominant hand above the other one in front of you, fingers pointing at opposite sides and palms touching.*

2 *Rotate your dominant hand clockwise then counter-clockwise, twice.*

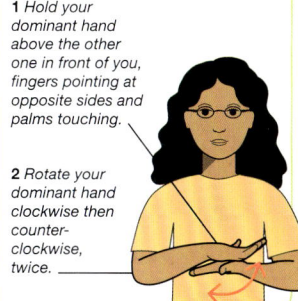

Yogurt

1 *Hold your dominant hand near your neck, facing you, with the thumb and little finger stuck out and the other fingers curled into a fist.*

2 *Bend and stick out your thumb, as if you are pressing a button. Do this several times.*

What is your favorite food?

Furrow your eyebrows.

1 *Hold your dominant hand in front of your chest, with the fingers together, the thumb extended, and the palm facing out. Push your hand forward.*

2 *Keep the hand relaxed near your face, with the middle finger bent in.*

Only the middle finger is bent.

3 *Move the hand back and forth so that you tap your chin with your middle finger, twice.*

Your

Favorite

I love pizza.

You can use this series of signs to express your love for other things, by using signs for a favorite food, person, or activity in place of "pizza."

2 *Curl in the index finger, and kiss the back of your hand.*

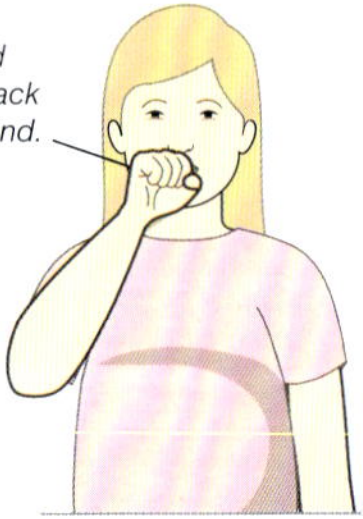

1 *Point the index finger of your dominant hand at your chest, with the rest of your fingers curled into a fist.*

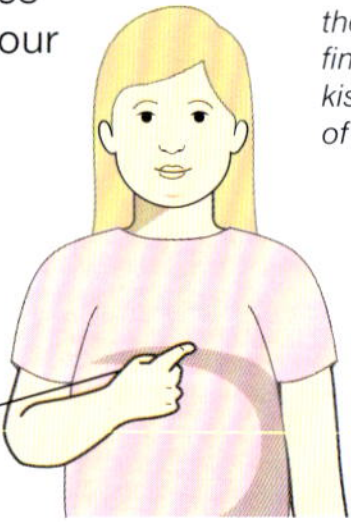

I

Love

Left hand
dominant

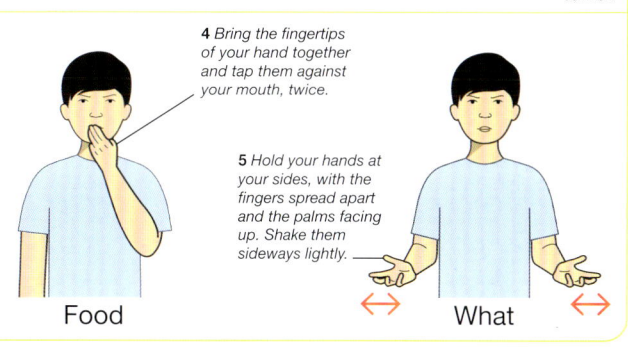

4 *Bring the fingertips of your hand together and tap them against your mouth, twice.*

Food

5 *Hold your hands at your sides, with the fingers spread apart and the palms facing up. Shake them sideways lightly.*

What

3 *Purse your mouth while pulling your hand away from it.*

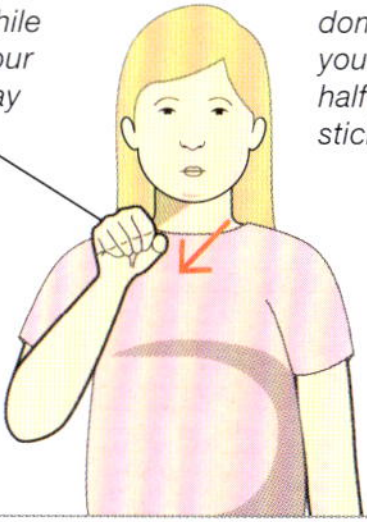

4 *Hold your dominant hand near your mouth, bent in half with the thumb sticking out.*

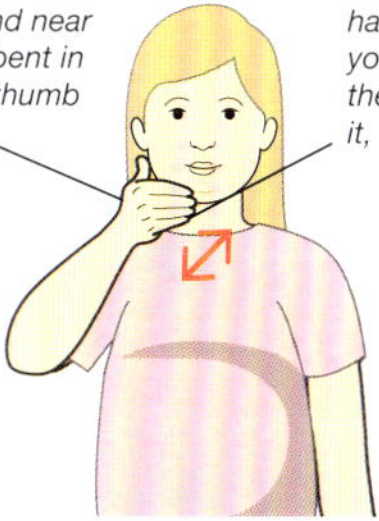

5 *Move your hand toward your mouth and then away from it, twice.*

Pizza

I'll make you a sandwich.

You can use this sentence to offer to make someone any type of food, by swapping in other words in place of "sandwich."

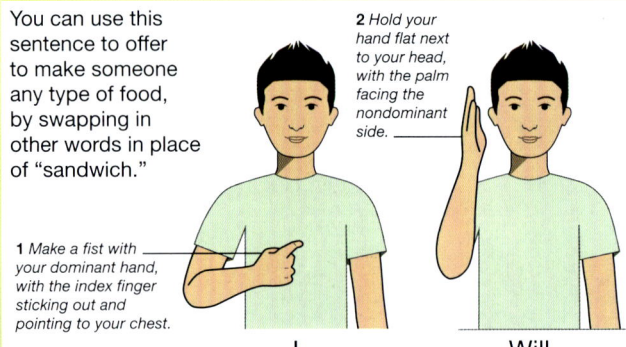

1 Make a fist with your dominant hand, with the index finger sticking out and pointing to your chest.

I

2 Hold your hand flat next to your head, with the palm facing the nondominant side.

Will

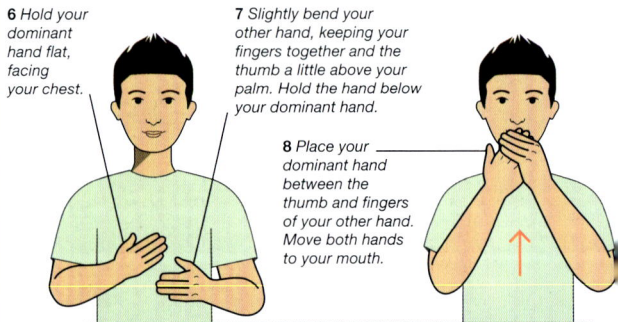

6 Hold your dominant hand flat, facing your chest.

7 Slightly bend your other hand, keeping your fingers together and the thumb a little above your palm. Hold the hand below your dominant hand.

8 Place your dominant hand between the thumb and fingers of your other hand. Move both hands to your mouth.

Sandwich

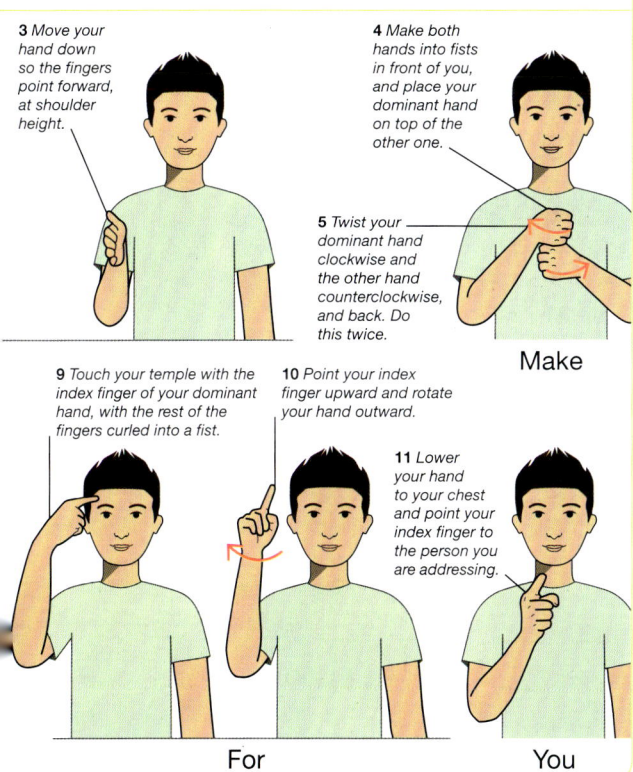

3 Move your hand down so the fingers point forward, at shoulder height.

4 Make both hands into fists in front of you, and place your dominant hand on top of the other one.

5 Twist your dominant hand clockwise and the other hand counterclockwise, and back. Do this twice.

Make

9 Touch your temple with the index finger of your dominant hand, with the rest of the fingers curled into a fist.

10 Point your index finger upward and rotate your hand outward.

11 Lower your hand to your chest and point your index finger to the person you are addressing.

For

You

I want an apple and an orange.

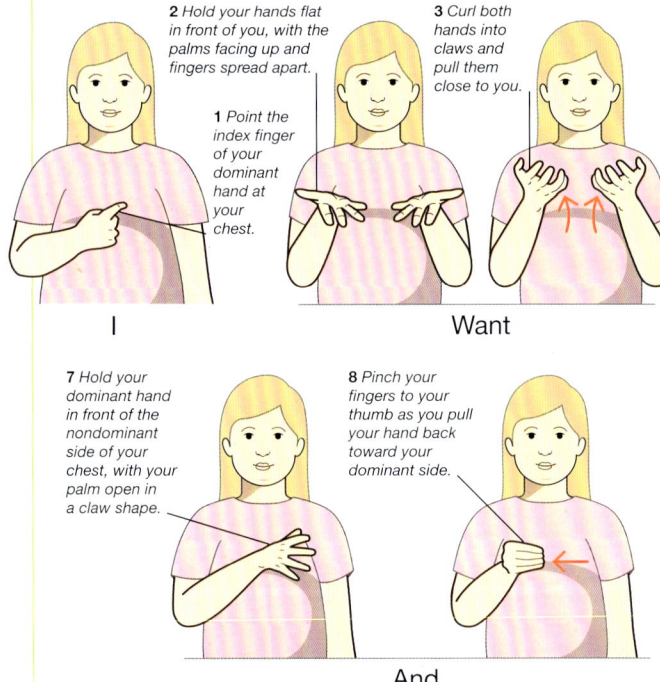

2 Hold your hands flat in front of you, with the palms facing up and fingers spread apart.

1 Point the index finger of your dominant hand at your chest.

3 Curl both hands into claws and pull them close to you.

I

Want

7 Hold your dominant hand in front of the nondominant side of your chest, with your palm open in a claw shape.

8 Pinch your fingers to your thumb as you pull your hand back toward your dominant side.

And

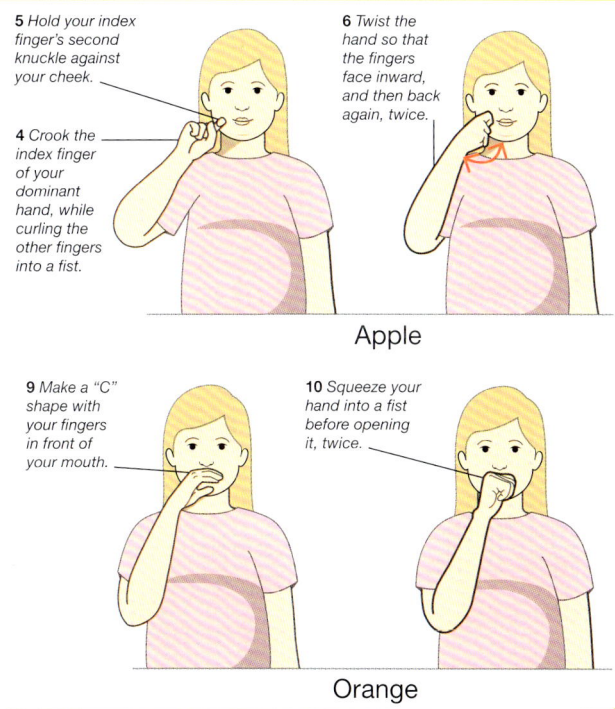

5 *Hold your index finger's second knuckle against your cheek.*

6 *Twist the hand so that the fingers face inward, and then back again, twice.*

4 *Crook the index finger of your dominant hand, while curling the other fingers into a fist.*

Apple

9 *Make a "C" shape with your fingers in front of your mouth.*

10 *Squeeze your hand into a fist before opening it, twice.*

Orange

I am allergic to nuts.

You can use this sentence to tell people that you have any other allergy, by swapping out the sign for "nuts."

Raise your eyebrows.

1 *Make a fist with your dominant hand facing forward, and hold it in front of you to your dominant side.*

2 *Bend the wrist forward and backward a few times, moving the fist up and down.*

Yes

Squint your eyes and curl your lips down.

4 *Touch the index finger of your dominant hand to your nose, while keeping the other fingers curled in a fist.*

5 *Point the index fingers of both hands at each other at chest height, with the rest of the fingers curled in.*

6 *Pull your hands away from each other.*

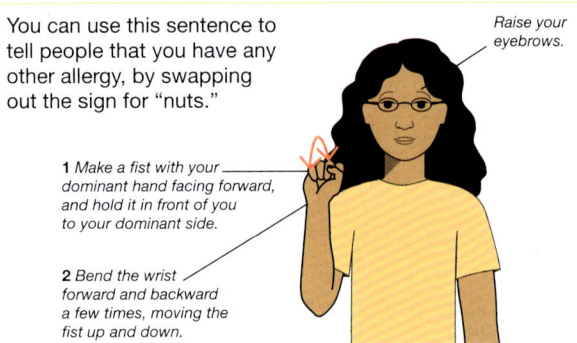

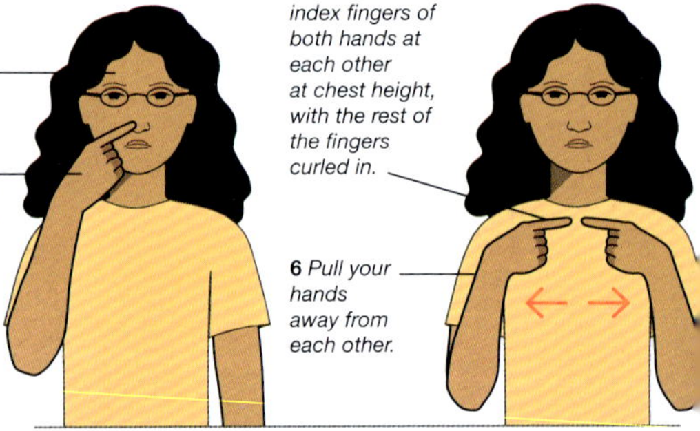

Allergy

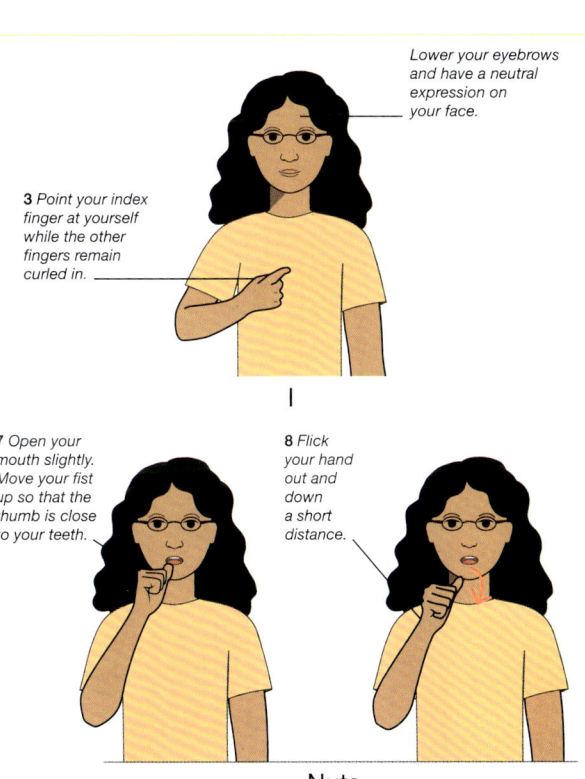

Lower your eyebrows and have a neutral expression on your face.

3 *Point your index finger at yourself while the other fingers remain curled in.*

I

7 *Open your mouth slightly. Move your fist up so that the thumb is close to your teeth.*

8 *Flick your hand out and down a short distance.*

Nuts

Would you like a drink?

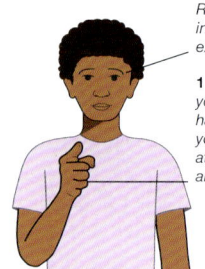

Raise your eyebrows in a questioning expression.

1 *Make a fist with your dominant hand, and point your index finger at the person you are talking to.*

You

2 *Hold both hands open, with the palms facing up and fingers stretched out in front of you.*

Want

A glass of water, please.

Nod your head throughout the sentence because you are answering a question.

2 *Curl your dominant hand, as if holding a glass, and place it on your other hand.*

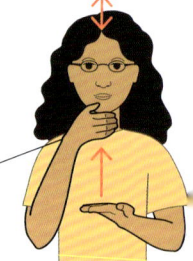

1 *Hold your nondominant hand flat in front of your chest, with the palm facing up.*

3 *Lift your dominant hand up to your face.*

Glass

3 *Curl your hands into claws and pull them toward yourself.*

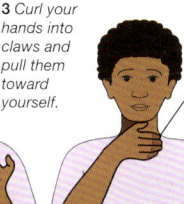

4 *Curl the fingers of your dominant hand in front of your mouth, as if holding a cup.*

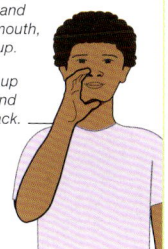

5 *Tilt your hand up to your mouth and tip your head back.*

Drink

4 *Hold the little finger of your dominant hand with your thumb in front of your face. Stick out the other fingers.*

5 *Tap your chin with your index finger, twice.*

The thumb touches the little finger's nail.

6 *Hold your dominant hand on your chest, with the thumb sticking out. Make clockwise circles.*

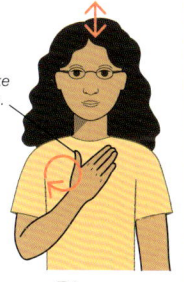

Water

Please

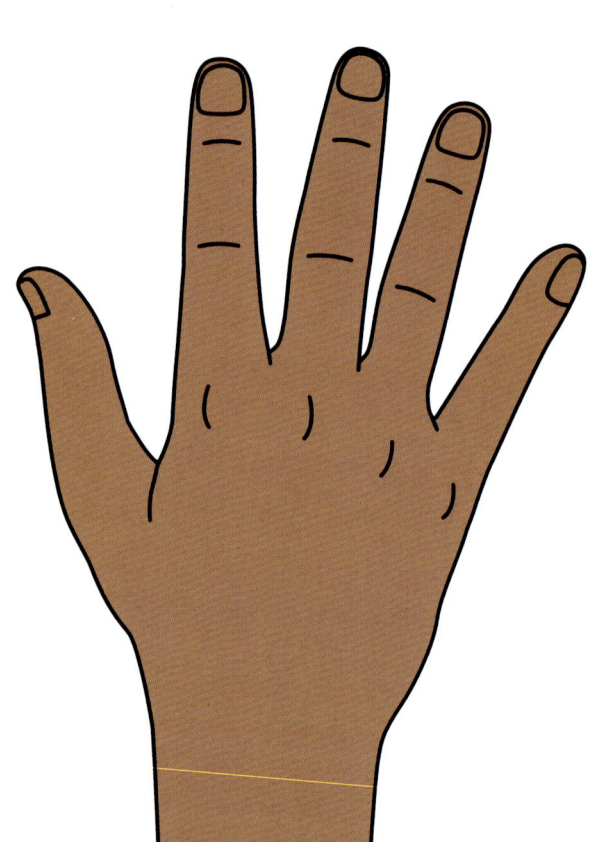

Chapter 5

SCHOOL AND ACTIVITIES

Here are some signs you will need to talk about school and the activities you might do. This includes school subjects, the people you might come across at school, and school activities, such as homework. Find also the signs for hobbies, such as dance, music, and painting.

◀ ASL sign for number 5

Read

2 *Stick out the index and middle fingers of your dominant hand in a "V" shape, and fold the other fingers into a fist.*

1 *Hold your nondominant hand upright and flat, with the fingers together, and turn it toward you slightly.*

TIP

Repeating the flicking movement of your dominant hand turns this sign into "reading."

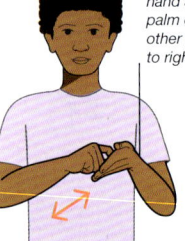

Write

2 *Touch the thumb of your dominant hand to your index finger, and fold the other fingers into a fist.*

3 *Drag the thumb and index finger of your dominant hand across the palm of your other hand, left to right, twice.*

1 *Hold your nondominant hand flat, with the palm facing you.*

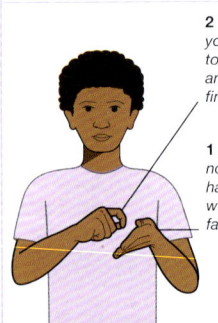

School

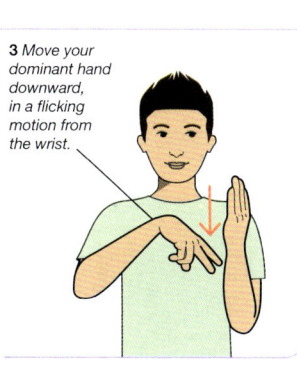

3 Move your dominant hand downward, in a flicking motion from the wrist.

1 Hold your dominant hand in front of you, with the palm facing the other one below it.

2 Strike the other hand with the dominant one a few times to clap.

Book

1 Join your palms in front of you, with your fingertips pointing away from you.

2 Open your hands with the palms facing up and make the two little fingers touch each other. Do this twice.

English

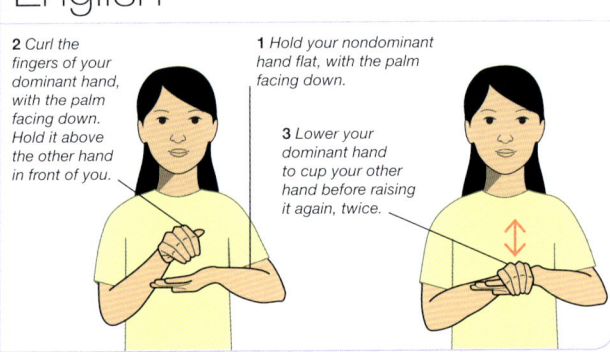

2 *Curl the fingers of your dominant hand, with the palm facing down. Hold it above the other hand in front of you.*

1 *Hold your nondominant hand flat, with the palm facing down.*

3 *Lower your dominant hand to cup your other hand before raising it again, twice.*

Science

1 *Make your hands into fists, with the thumbs sticking out. Hold the dominant hand up, with the fist facing out.*

2 *Keep the other hand across the belly, with thumb facing down.*

3 *Make half circles with your hands, one after another, as if you are pouring water into a container. Do this twice.*

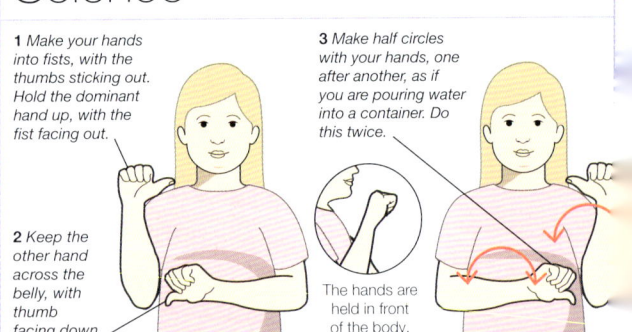

The hands are held in front of the body.

History

Left hand
dominant

1 *Hold your dominant hand in front of you. Stick out your index and middle fingers, with the other fingers curled in.*

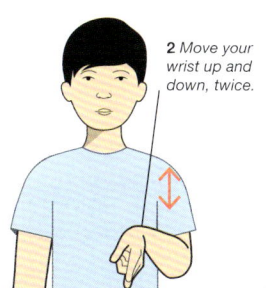

2 *Move your wrist up and down, twice.*

Math

1 *Fold in the little fingers and thumbs of your hands while bending the other fingers.*

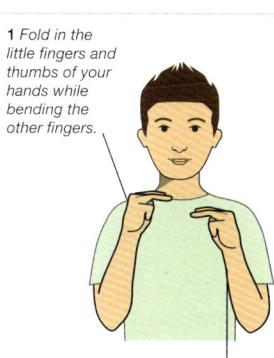

2 *Hold your hands in front of you, facing each other, with the dominant hand held slightly higher.*

3 *Move your hands toward each other and back, crossing your wrists a few times.*

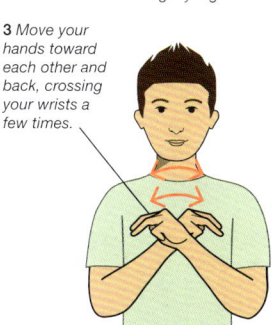

Teacher

This sign is a combination of the signs for the words "teach" and "person."

1 Curl your fingers and thumbs together and hold both hands near your temples.

2 Move your hands away from your head, then swing them forward.

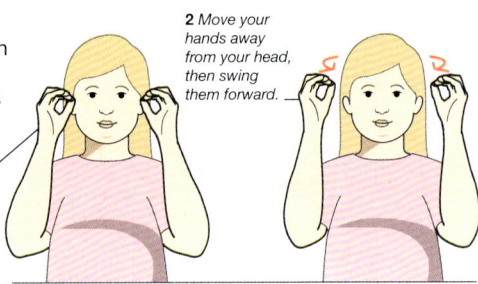

Teach

Class

1 Curl both your hands into "C" shapes, with the palms facing away from you. Hold them in front of your chest.

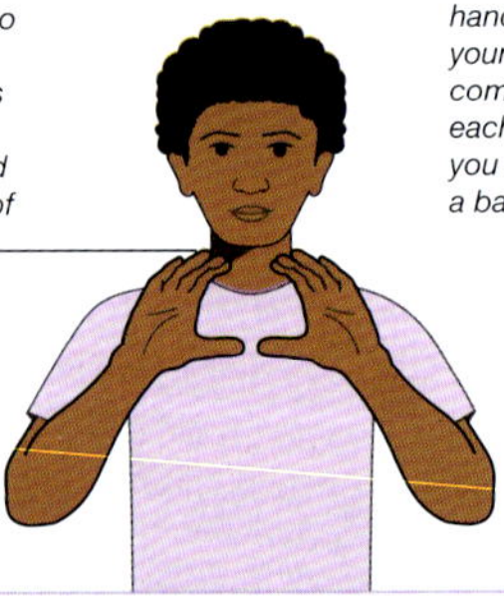

2 Turn your hands until your little fingers come close to each other, as if you are creating a ball.

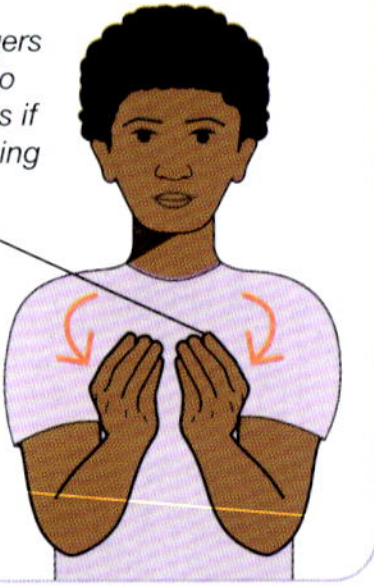

3 *Hold your arms in front of your chest. Open the palms to face each other.*

4 *Keeping them the same distance apart, move the hands down toward your abdomen.*

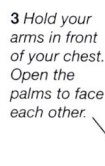

Person

Test

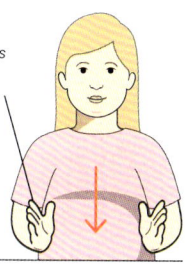

Left hand dominant

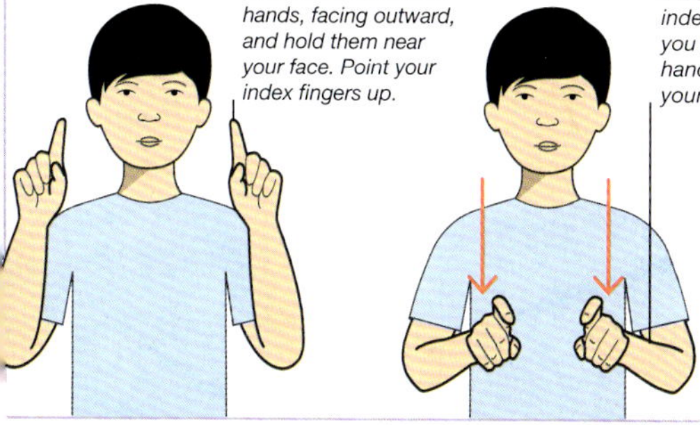

1 *Make fists with both hands, facing outward, and hold them near your face. Point your index fingers up.*

2 *Bend the index fingers as you move the hands down to your abdomen.*

Homework

1 *Bring the fingers of your dominant hand together and touch the fingertips to your cheek.*

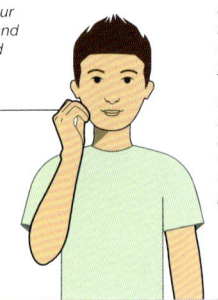

3 *Make a fist with your dominant hand and lower it until its wrist touches the side of your other fist.*

2 *Curl your nondominant hand into a fist in front of your chest, with the thumb pointing down.*

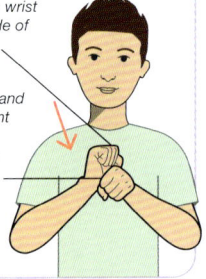

Coach

1 *Curl the fingers of your dominant hand in a cupping gesture. Place them on your shoulder.*

2 *Tap your shoulder with your hand, twice.*

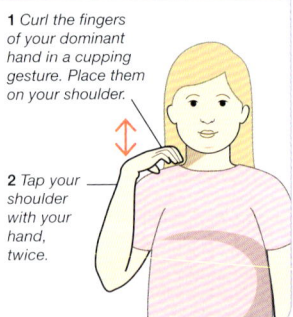

Student

2 *Bring the fingertips of your dominant hand together. Place them on your other hand.*

1 *Hold your nondominant hand flat in front of you, with the palm facing up.*

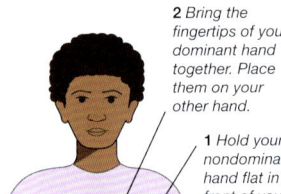

Study

2 *Hold your dominant hand open and relaxed over your other hand and wiggle the fingers.*

1 *Place your nondominant hand flat in front of you, with the palm facing up and toward you.*

Gym

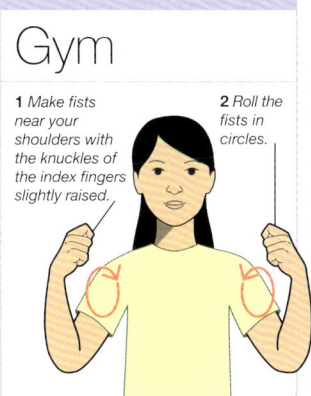

1 *Make fists near your shoulders with the knuckles of the index fingers slightly raised.*

2 *Roll the fists in circles.*

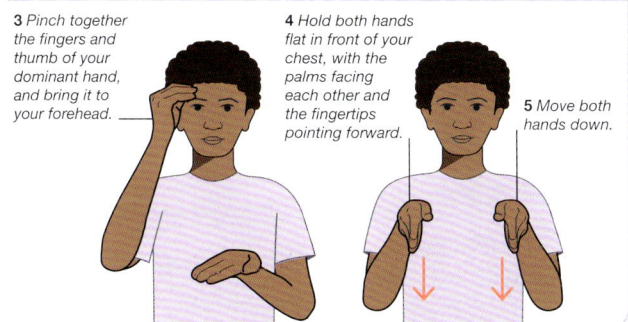

3 *Pinch together the fingers and thumb of your dominant hand, and bring it to your forehead.*

4 *Hold both hands flat in front of your chest, with the palms facing each other and the fingertips pointing forward.*

5 *Move both hands down.*

Win

1 *Hold your dominant hand in front of your upper chest, with the fingers spread apart and slightly curled.*

3 *Tap the nondominant hand with your dominant one. Curl your dominant hand into a fist as you move it back up.*

2 *Hold your other hand in a fist in front of your lower chest.*

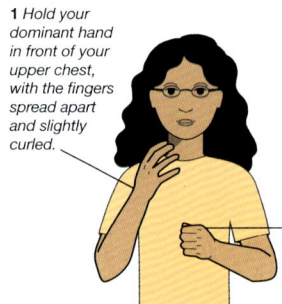
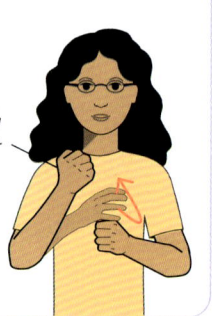

Lose

Furrow your eyebrows and turn down the corners of your mouth.

3 *Bring your dominant hand down so that its fingers touch the palm of the other hand.*

2 *Hold your dominant hand up, then stick out your index and middle fingers in a "V" shape, with the other fingers curled in.*

1 *Place your nondominant hand in front of your chest, with the palm facing up and fingers together.*

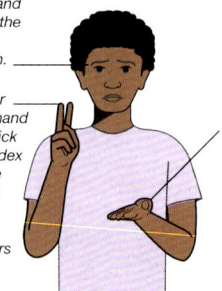
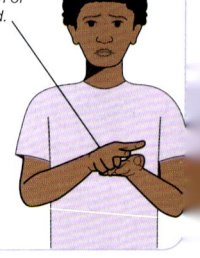

Play

1 *Make fists with your hands in front of your chest, facing down, with the thumbs and little fingers sticking out. Point the thumbs toward your chest.*

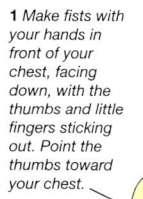

2 *Swing your hands inward from the wrists, moving the little fingers close to each other and then back. Do this twice.*

Game

1 *Curl the fingers of your hands into fists, with the thumbs sticking up.*

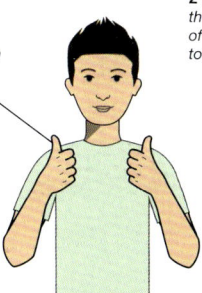

2 *Touch the knuckles of both hands together, twice.*

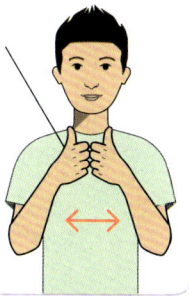

Football

1 *Hold your hands in front of you, with the palms facing each other and the fingers spread apart.*

2 *Bring your hands together and interlock your fingers, twice.*

Soccer

1 *Hold your nondominant hand flat in front of you, with the palm facing the side and fingers pointing up.*

2 *Hold your dominant hand lower than the other hand, bent at the wrist and with the palm facing in and the fingers pointing down.*

3 *Bring the dominant hand up to knock at the side of the other hand, twice.*

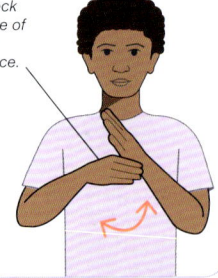

Hockey

2 Keep your dominant hand in a fist facing up, but with your index finger curled and not folded in.

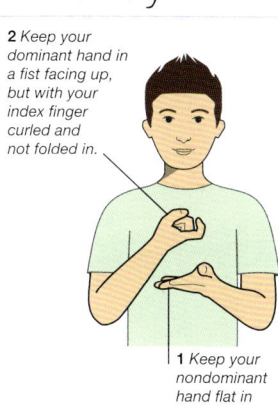

1 Keep your nondominant hand flat in front of you, with the palm facing up.

3 Sweep the curled index finger across the flat palm of the other hand toward your chest, twice.

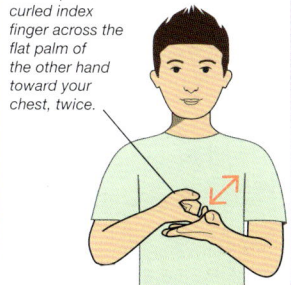

Baseball

1 Make both hands into fists, and hold them in front of your dominant shoulder, with the dominant fist stacked on top of the other one.

2 Keep your fists together and swing them a short distance away from you and then back, twice.

TIP

Imagine you are holding a baseball bat and getting ready to make a strike.

Walking

1 *Hold your hands flat in front of you, with the palms facing down.*

2 *Move your hands forward and backward, one at a time, so that they look like feet walking.*

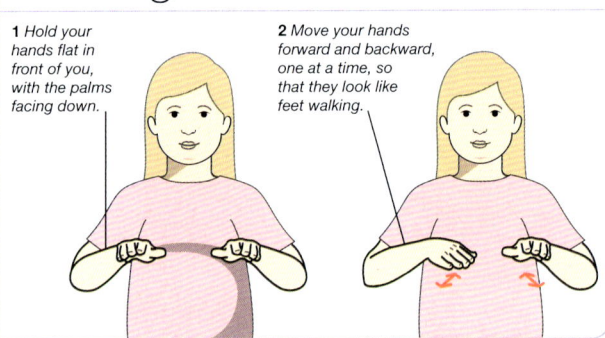

Dancing

2 *Curl your dominant hand into a fist, but stick out the index and middle fingers, keeping them slightly apart. Bend your wrist and hold the fingers over the palm of your other hand.*

1 *Hold your nondominant hand flat in front of your chest, with the palm facing up.*

3 *Swing the extended fingers back and forth over the open palm— like legs on a dance floor.*

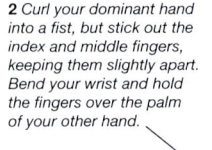

Biking

1 *Make both hands into fists and hold them in front of you, one above the other.*

2 *Make circles in front of you, moving each hand forward after the other, as if pedaling a bike.*

Skateboarding

Left hand dominant

1 *Keep your hands in front of you. Curl in the fingers of both hands. Hold the ring and little fingers down with your thumb.*

2 *Hold your dominant hand a little farther away from you than the other hand. Move both hands back and forth, twice.*

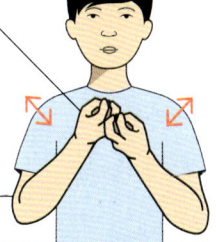

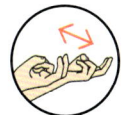

The hands move down when going forward and up when going backward.

Movie

1 *Hold your dominant hand upright, with the fingers slightly spread apart.*

2 *Keep the nondominant hand's fingers together and place it sideways across the dominant hand. Bring the palms together.*

3 *Wave the fingers of your dominant hand a few times.*

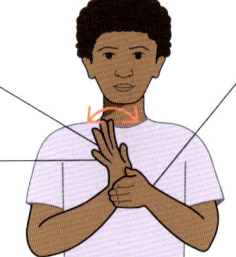

TIP

You can also make this sign with your nondominant hand held flat, palm facing down.

Travel

1 *Make a claw with your dominant hand in front of you, curling your index and middle fingers and tucking in the other fingers and thumb.*

2 *Make two circles while swinging the hand outward to the side.*

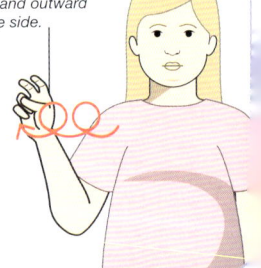

Music

Left hand dominant

2 *Hold up your dominant hand flat, with your palm facing the other side. Sweep your hand back and forth over your other hand.*

1 *Bend your nondominant hand in front of you, with the palm facing up.*

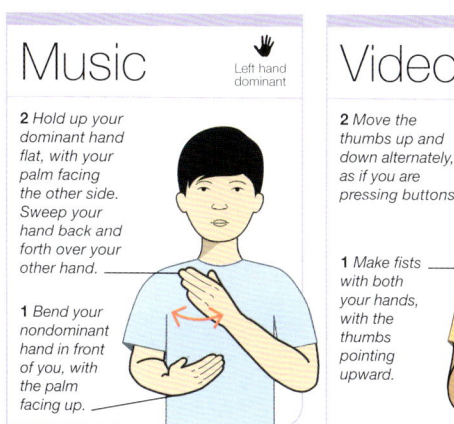

Video games

2 *Move the thumbs up and down alternately, as if you are pressing buttons.*

1 *Make fists with both your hands, with the thumbs pointing upward.*

Painting

1 *Hold up your nondominant hand with the palm facing the other side. Touch its fingers with those of your dominant hand.*

2 *Move the fingers of your dominant hand down your other hand and then back up again a few times.*

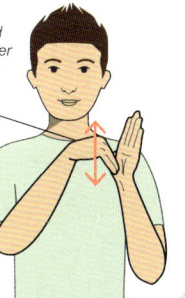

My favorite class is math.

In ASL, expressions are also used to draw attention to the main topic of a sentence. Here, the raised eyebrows tell us that the topic is "math."

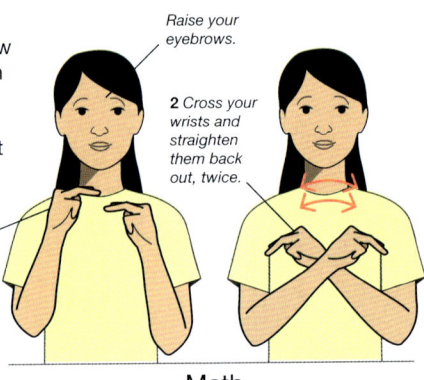

Raise your eyebrows.

2 *Cross your wrists and straighten them back out, twice.*

1 *Cross the thumbs of both hands over the little fingers, and stretch the other fingers toward each other. Hold your dominant hand a bit higher than the other one in front of you.*

Math

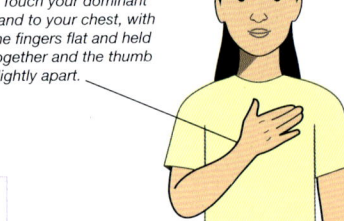

5 *Touch your dominant hand to your chest, with the fingers flat and held together and the thumb slightly apart.*

My

TIP

Use fisted hands in steps 1 and 2, with the thumbs on the outside, to change the sign to "algebra."

3 Loosely curl both hands in front of you, with the palms facing out.

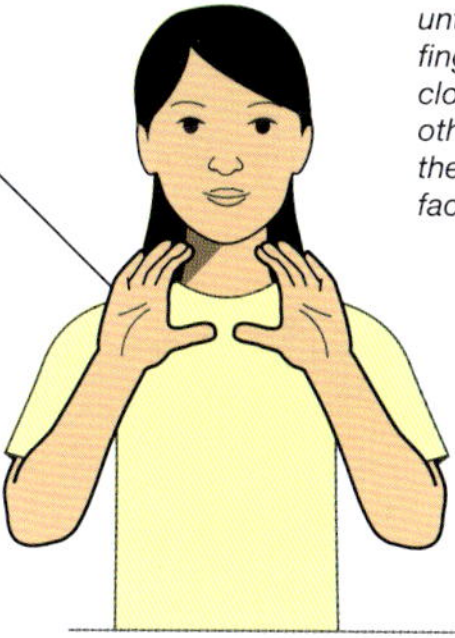

4 Circle your hands forward until the little fingers come close to each other and the palms face inward.

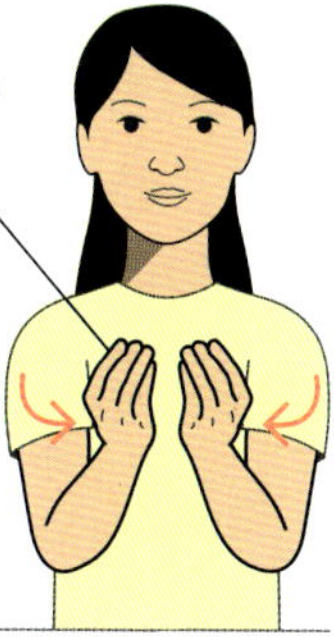

Class

6 Stretch out the fingers of your dominant hand, with the middle finger bent to point at your chin.

7 Move the hand back and forth so that you tap your chin with your middle finger, twice.

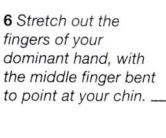

Favorite

Only the middle finger touches the chin.

Have you done your homework?

In this sentence, the English word "done" has been signed as "finish" because we are talking about finishing a task.

Raise your eyebrows in a questioning expression.

1 *Touch the fingertips of your dominant hand together and hold them to the side of your face.*

Homework

4 *Point the index finger of your dominant hand at the person you are talking to, with the rest of the fingers curled into a fist.*

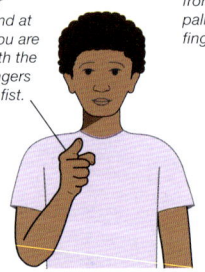

You

5 *Hold both hands in front of you, with the palms facing you and fingers spread apart.*

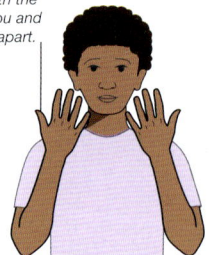

Finish

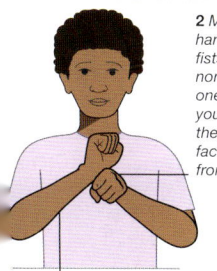

2 *Make both hands into fists. Hold the nondominant one in front of your chest, with the knuckles facing away from you.*

3 *Stack the wrist of the dominant hand on the other hand's fist, with the palm facing outward and slightly away from you.*

6 *Turn your hands around so that the palms face away from you.*

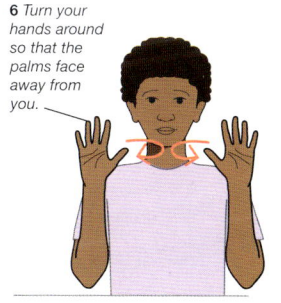

Not yet.

Shake your head from side to side while signing.

Open your mouth and hold your tongue over your bottom teeth.

1 *Hold your dominant hand at your side. Bend it down from the wrist, palm facing inward, with the fingers together and thumb sticking out.*

2 *Move your hand forward and backward a few times.*

The hand bends at the wrist when it moves.

Do you play basketball?

This question could also be the other way around, as "Basketball you play?"

Raise both your eyebrows.

1 *Make your dominant hand into a fist, with the index finger pointing at the person you are talking to.*

2 *Make both hands into fists in front of your chest, facing down, with the little fingers and thumbs sticking out. Point the thumbs toward your chest.*

4 *Fold your ring and little fingers in, and slightly curl in the other fingers. Point the index fingers forward while the palms face each other.*

5 *Twist your hands up, down, and then up again.*

You

Play

Basketball

Sometimes.

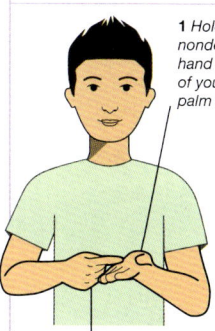

1 *Hold your nondominant hand flat in front of you, with the palm facing up.*

2 *Make your dominant hand into a fist, but stick out the index finger and place it on the other palm.*

3 *Twist your hands inward from the wrists, moving the little fingers close to each and then back, twice.*

3 *Tap your dominant hand's index finger on the palm of your other hand, then raise it to draw a circle in front of you, twice.*

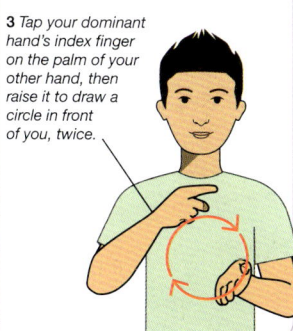

TIP

To remember this sign, imagine you are holding a ball and getting ready to throw it.

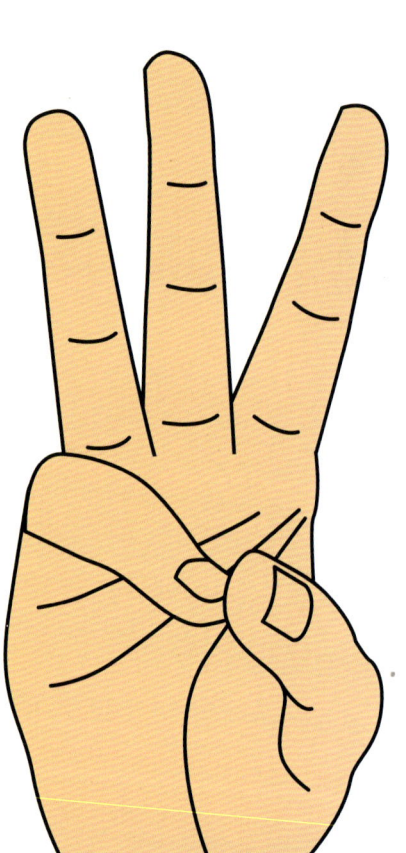

Chapter 6

NATURE

What can you see around you when you go outdoors?
There is a sign for everything, whether it is the sun,
the moon, the sky, a mountain, the ocean, or even the
"outside." There are signs for the weather, too.

◄ ASL sign for number 6

Outdoors

1 *Make a claw shape with your dominant hand and hold it at the side of your head.*

2 *Bring your fingertips together as you pull your hand away from your head, before moving your hand back and opening your fingers again. Do this twice.*

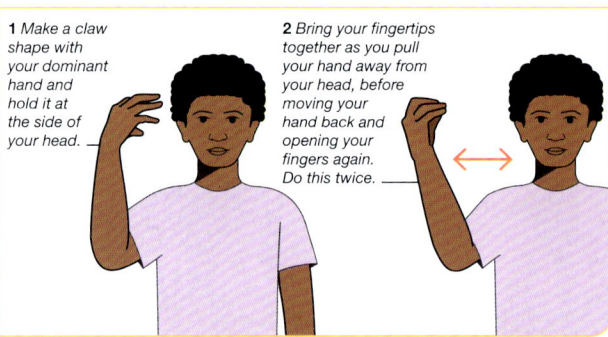

River

1 *Hold the little finger of your dominant hand down with the thumb. Stick out the other fingers in a "W" shape and touch the index finger to your chin.*

2 *Place both hands flat in front of you, their palms facing each other.*

3 *Curve your hands from side to side, away from you, like a flowing river.*

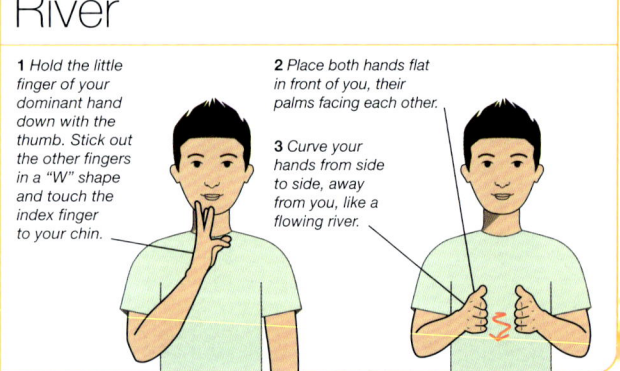

Mountain

2 Hold your dominant hand in a fist above your other hand.

3 Knock your dominant hand against the back of your other hand.

1 Make a fist with your nondominant hand in front of your chest, with the fingers facing down.

4 Open both fists, keeping the palms facing down, and move your hands upward and toward your dominant side.

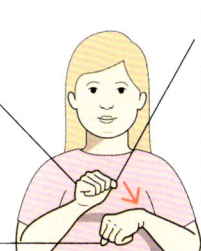
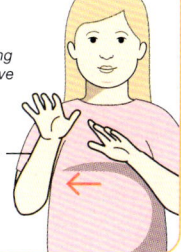

Ocean

1 Hold both hands relaxed in front of you, with the fingers spread apart and palms facing away from you.

2 Move your hands up and down twice in a wavelike motion, forward and away from you.

The hands imitate the motion of waves.

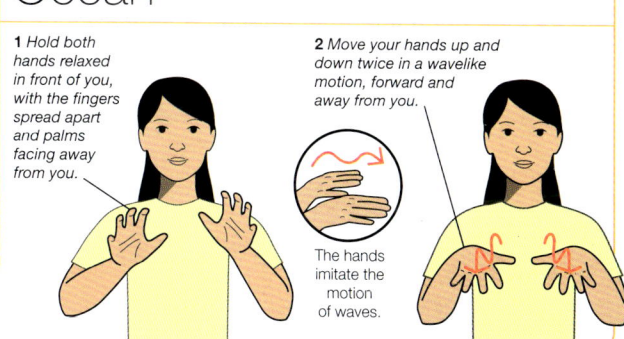

Tree

2 *Hold up your dominant hand, with the palm facing you. Spread the fingers and place your elbow on your other hand.*

3 *Wiggle your dominant hand at the wrist, twice.*

1 *Place your nondominant arm across your body, with the palm flat and facing down.*

TIP

Your dominant hand sways like a tree in the wind, while your other hand mimics the ground.

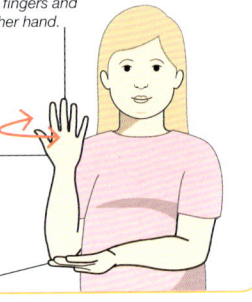

Flower

1 *Bend your dominant hand to bring the fingers and thumb together. Bring your hand up to touch the side of your nose.*

2 *Keep your hand as it is and move it across to touch the other side of your nose.*

Forest

1 *Turn slightly toward your nondominant side.*

3 *Hold your dominant hand in front of you, palm facing inward and fingers spread out, with the elbow resting on your other arm.*

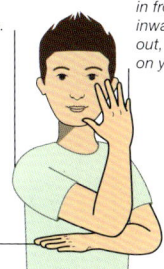

2 *Place your nondominant arm across your body, with the palm flat and facing down.*

4 *Move your arms toward your dominant side, while wiggling your dominant hand at the wrist a few times.*

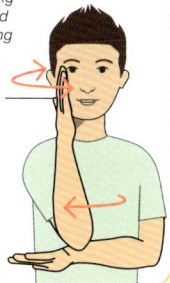

Butterfly

1 *Hold your hands up in front of you, with the palms flat and facing you. Cross your hands and interlock your thumbs.*

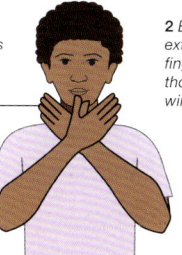

2 *Bend and extend your fingers, twice, as though they are wings in flight.*

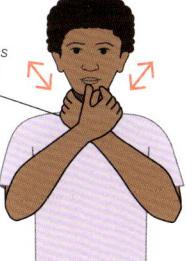

Sky

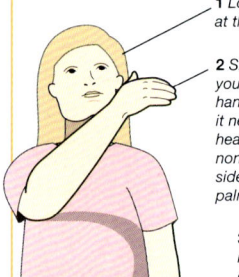

1 *Look up at the sky.*

2 *Slightly curve your dominant hand. Hold it near your head on your nondominant side, with the palm facing in.*

3 *Move your hand in an arc to your dominant side.*

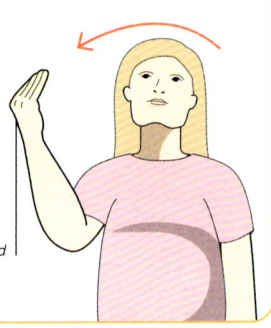

Moon

1 *Make a fist with your dominant hand, curling the index finger and thumb into a "C" shape near your eye.*

2 *Move your hand up and away from your head.*

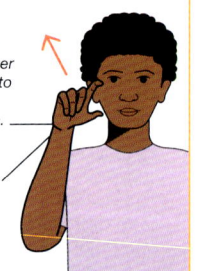

Sun

1 *Hold your dominant hand at the side of your head, with the palm facing out and up, and the fingers slightly curved.*

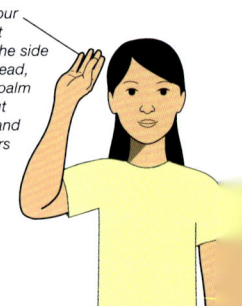

Star

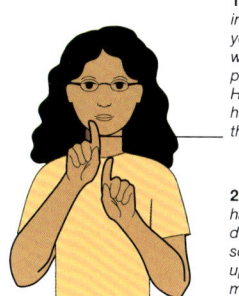

1 *Make both hands into fists in front of you, facing forward, with the index fingers pointing upward. Hold your dominant hand a little higher than the other one.*

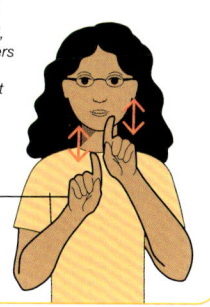

2 *Move your hands up and down repeatedly so that one moves up while the other moves down.*

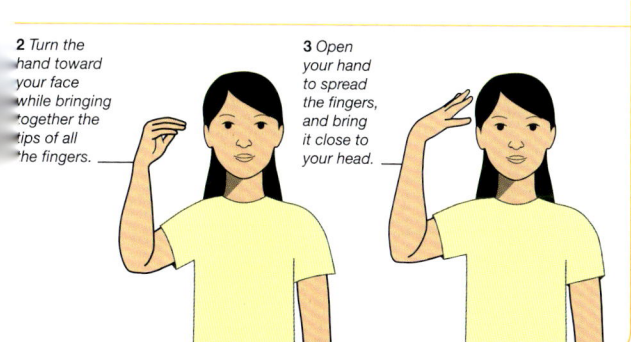

2 *Turn the hand toward your face while bringing together the tips of all the fingers.*

3 *Open your hand to spread the fingers, and bring it close to your head.*

Rain

Purse your lips.

1 Hold both hands in front of your chest, with the fingers forming a claw shape and the palms facing down.

2 Move your hands slightly up and down from the wrist, twice.

Snow

1 Hold both hands in front of your shoulders, with your fingers spread and the palms facing down.

2 Wiggle your fingers and bring your hands down slowly.

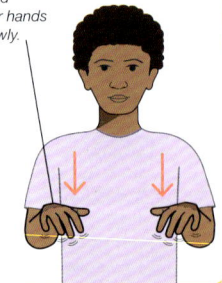

Cloud

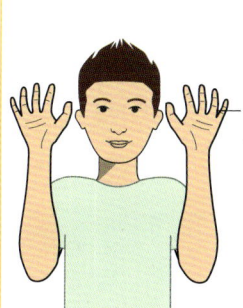

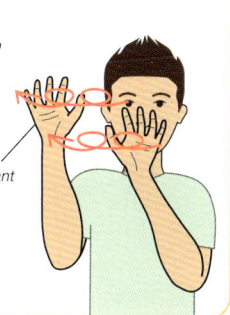

1 *Slightly curve both hands, palms facing diagonally up and forward, and hold them on either side of your head.*

2 *Move both hands toward your dominant side, while making little circles.*

Wind

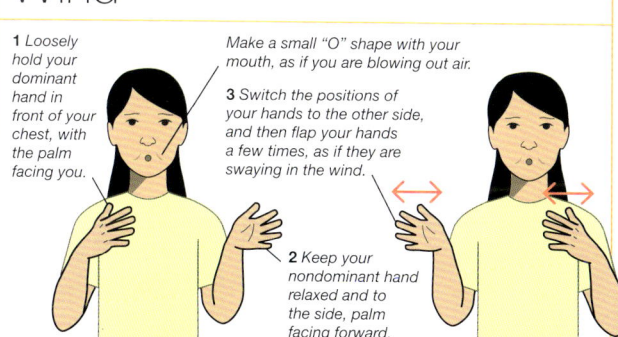

1 *Loosely hold your dominant hand in front of your chest, with the palm facing you.*

Make a small "O" shape with your mouth, as if you are blowing out air.

3 *Switch the positions of your hands to the other side, and then flap your hands a few times, as if they are swaying in the wind.*

2 *Keep your nondominant hand relaxed and to the side, palm facing forward.*

Is it very sunny outside?

1 Hold your dominant hand at the side of your head, with the palm facing out and up, and the fingers slightly curved.

Sunny

4 Bring the dominant hand next to your head, with the fingers slightly curled in and the palm facing you.

5 Pinch your fingers together and move the hand a little away from your head.

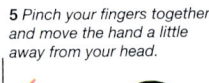

Outside

2 *Turn the hand toward your face while bringing together the tips of all the fingers.*

3 *Flare out the fingers of your hand as you bring it in front of your face.*

6 *Open the hand slightly and bring it closer to your face.*

Raise your eyebrows in a questioning expression.

8 *Make a fist with your hand, with the index finger pointing upward.*

7 *Pinch the fingers together and move the hand away from you.*

9 *Bend and then stick out your index finger, twice.*

?

It's dark and windy this evening.

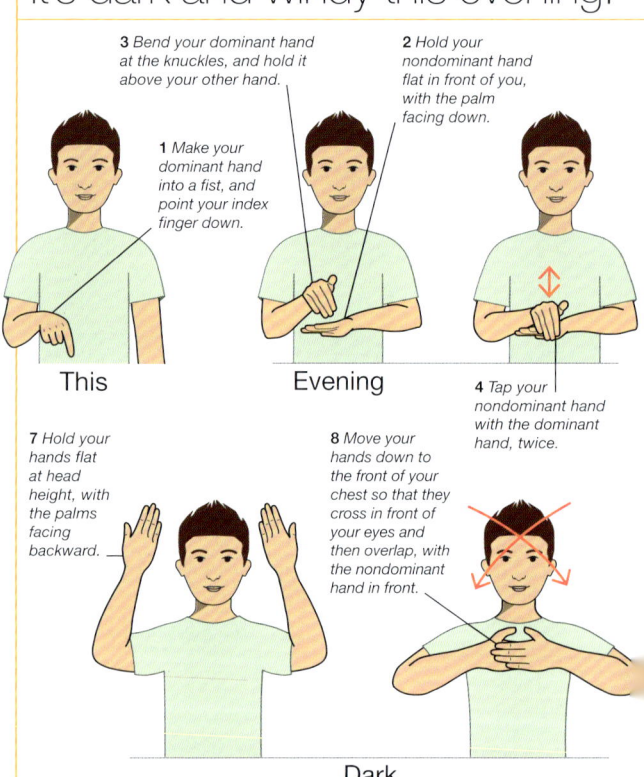

3 *Bend your dominant hand at the knuckles, and hold it above your other hand.*

1 *Make your dominant hand into a fist, and point your index finger down.*

2 *Hold your nondominant hand flat in front of you, with the palm facing down.*

This

Evening

4 *Tap your nondominant hand with the dominant hand, twice.*

7 *Hold your hands flat at head height, with the palms facing backward.*

8 *Move your hands down to the front of your chest so that they cross in front of your eyes and then overlap, with the nondominant hand in front.*

Dark

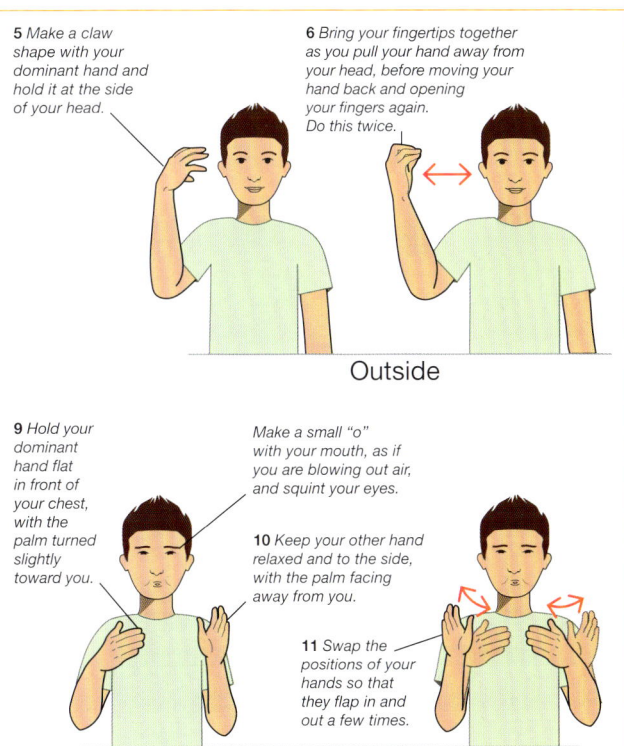

5 Make a claw shape with your dominant hand and hold it at the side of your head.

6 Bring your fingertips together as you pull your hand away from your head, before moving your hand back and opening your fingers again. Do this twice.

Outside

9 Hold your dominant hand flat in front of your chest, with the palm turned slightly toward you.

Make a small "o" with your mouth, as if you are blowing out air, and squint your eyes.

10 Keep your other hand relaxed and to the side, with the palm facing away from you.

11 Swap the positions of your hands so that they flap in and out a few times.

Windy

Summer is my favorite season.

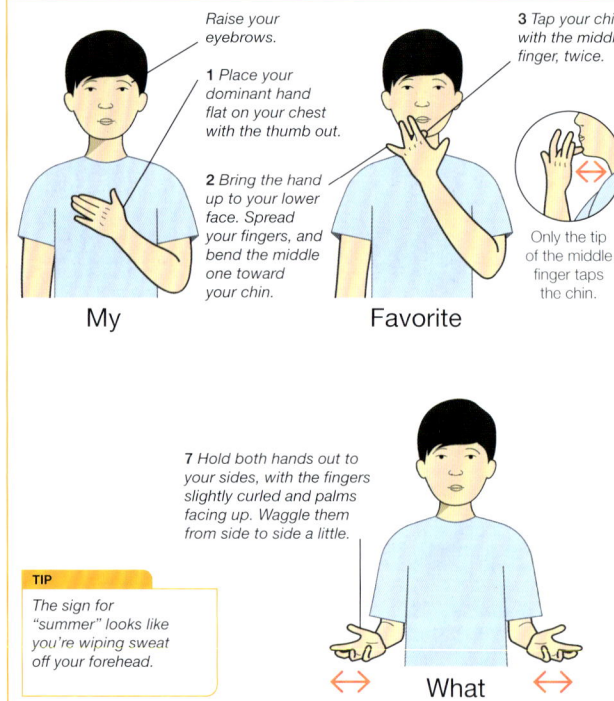

Raise your eyebrows.

1 *Place your dominant hand flat on your chest with the thumb out.*

2 *Bring the hand up to your lower face. Spread your fingers, and bend the middle one toward your chin.*

My

3 *Tap your chin with the middle finger, twice.*

Only the tip of the middle finger taps the chin.

Favorite

7 *Hold both hands out to your sides, with the fingers slightly curled and palms facing up. Waggle them from side to side a little.*

What

TIP
The sign for "summer" looks like you're wiping sweat off your forehead.

Left hand
dominant

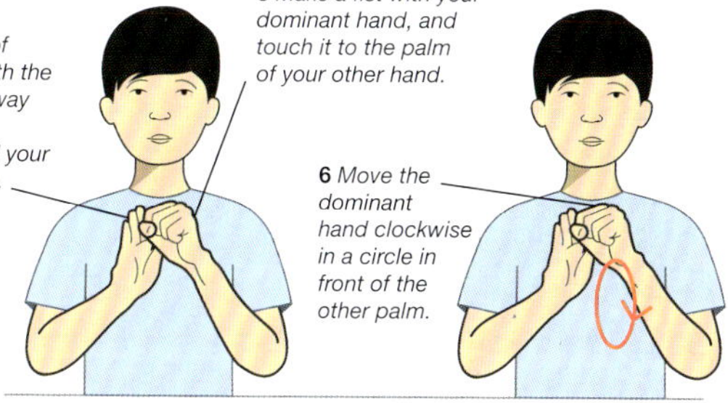

4 Hold your nondominant hand in front of your chest, with the palm facing away from you and slightly toward your dominant side.

5 Make a fist with your dominant hand, and touch it to the palm of your other hand.

6 Move the dominant hand clockwise in a circle in front of the other palm.

Season

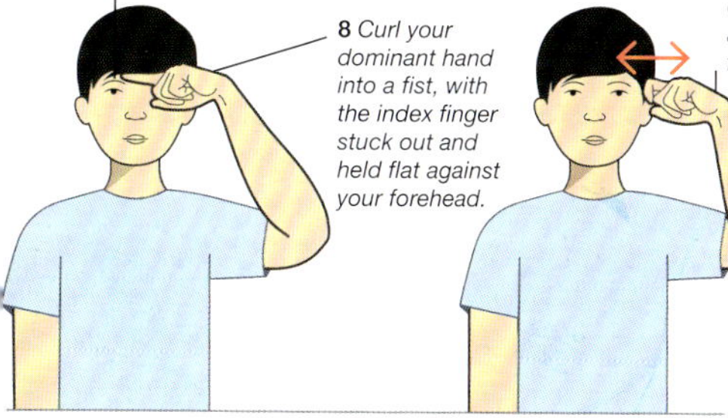

Lower your eyebrows and have a neutral expression.

8 Curl your dominant hand into a fist, with the index finger stuck out and held flat against your forehead.

9 Bend the index finger in half and drag it backward along your forehead, twice.

Summer

Chapter 7

ACTION AND DESCRIPTIVE WORDS

Many words are used to describe actions and movements. Some of them express physical movements, such as "run" or "jump," while others describe thinking actions, such as "remember" and "forget." In ASL, some action words, such as "go" and "come," can also be used to show direction of movement.

◀ ASL sign for number 7

Come

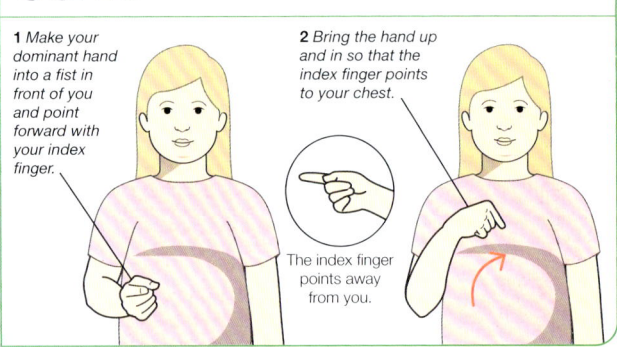

1 *Make your dominant hand into a fist in front of you and point forward with your index finger.*

2 *Bring the hand up and in so that the index finger points to your chest.*

The index finger points away from you.

Move

1 *Bend both your hands at the knuckles, with the fingers straight and close together.*

2 *Keep your dominant arm in front of your chest with the fingers pointing toward the nondominant side.*

4 *Move both hands toward your dominant side.*

3 *Hold your other hand at your side with the fingers pointing forward.*

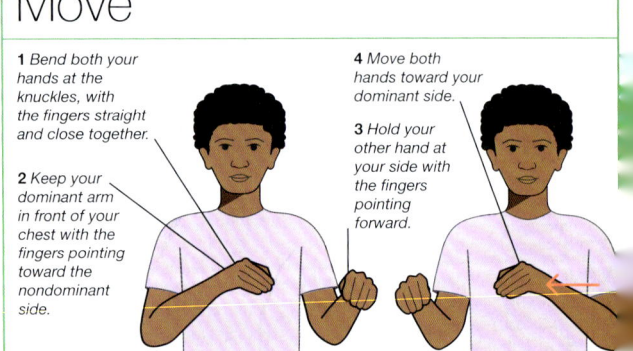

Go

1 *Spread the fingers of your dominant hand, and hold it in front of your chest, with the palm facing you.*

2 *Bring your fingers together while pulling your hand away from you.*

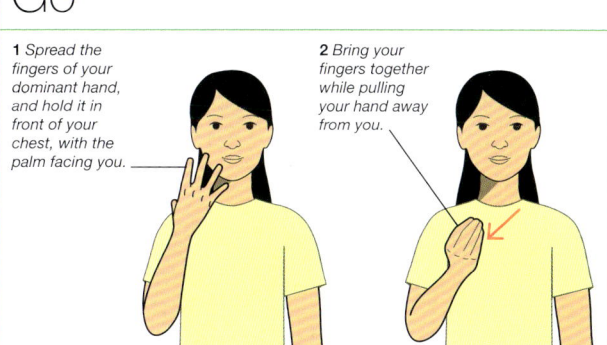

Stay

1 *Make fists with your hands in front of your chest, palms facing down. Stick out your little fingers and thumbs.*

2 *Move both hands down and slightly forward.*

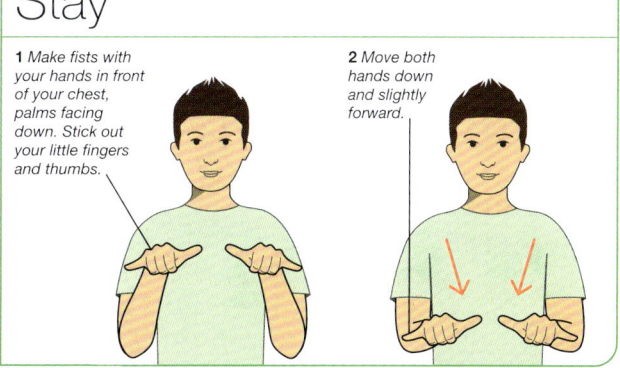

Fall

2 *Make a fist with your dominant hand, and hold it over the other hand. Stick out its index and middle fingers to touch the other palm.*

3 *Twist your dominant hand so that the extended fingers fall back on the open palm and the curled fingers face up.*

1 *Hold your nondominant hand flat in front of your belly, with the palm facing up.*

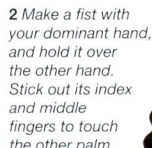

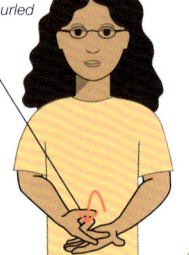

Run

The English word "run" can have many different meanings. This ASL sign is used for the word "run" as in "to move faster than walking."

1 *Hold both hands at around shoulder height near your nondominant side, with the index fingers and thumbs stuck out and the other fingers curled in.*

2 *Hook the index finger of your dominant hand around the thumb of your nondominant hand.*

Top view of hands being hooked together

Jump

Left hand dominant

1 *Hold your nondominant hand flat in front of your chest, with the palm facing up.*

3 *Raise your dominant hand, curling your index and middle fingers slightly. Then bring it back down, with the fingers stuck out. Do this twice.*

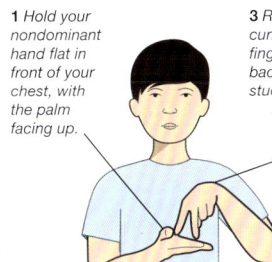

2 *Make a fist with your dominant hand, but extend its index and middle fingers down to touch the other palm.*

3 *Bend and then stick out your nondominant hand's index finger while moving both hands away from your body.*

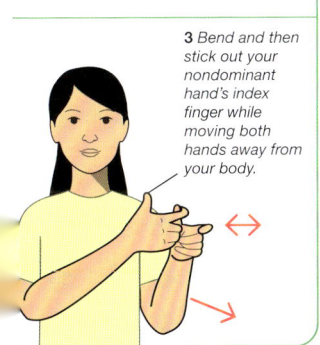

Climb

1 *Make both hands into claw shapes in front of you, with the palms facing away from you.*

2 *Move your hands up and back down, one at a time, as if you are climbing a ladder.*

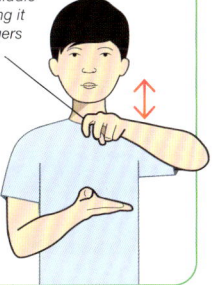

Catch

This is one way of signing "catch," often used for baseball.

1 *Hold your dominant hand in front of you, with the palm facing forward and the fingers spread and slightly curled.*

2 *Make a fist with your nondominant hand.*

3 *Bring the fist up and wrap the curled hand around it, as though it has caught a ball.*

4 *Tilt your body slightly toward your dominant side.*

Throw

1 *Curl your fingers into your palm, holding the fingernails of the index and middle fingers with your thumb.*

2 *Look toward your dominant side.*

3 *Stick out your index and middle fingers, and move your hand downward as if you are throwing something.*

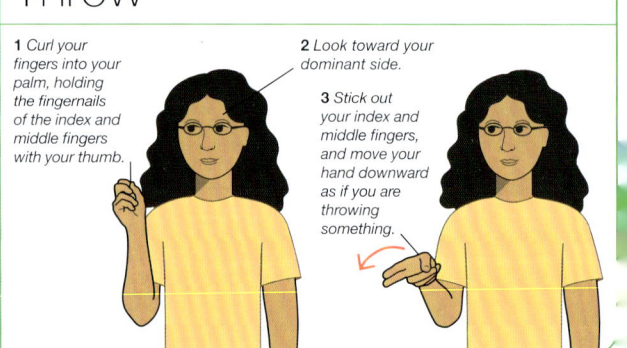

Give

1 *Place your dominant hand in front of your chest, with the* *palm facing up. Touch the thumb with the fingertips.*

2 *Move your hand away from your body, as though you are giving something to someone.*

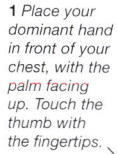

Take

1 *Spread the fingers of your dominant hand, with the palm facing down. Move it toward your dominant side.*

2 *Look toward your dominant side.*

3 *Draw your hand back to your chest and close it into a fist as you look in front.*

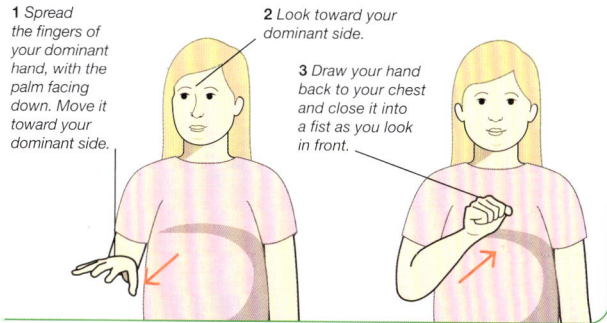

Listen

Left hand dominant

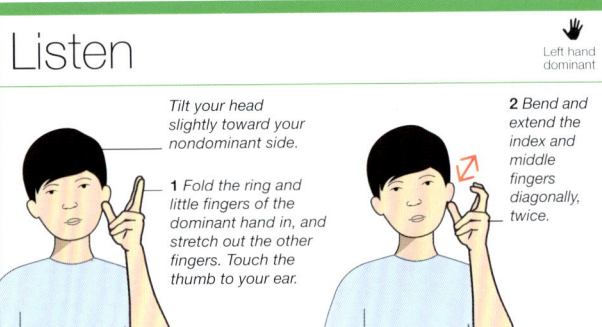

Tilt your head slightly toward your nondominant side.

1 *Fold the ring and little fingers of the dominant hand in, and stretch out the other fingers. Touch the thumb to your ear.*

2 *Bend and extend the index and middle fingers diagonally, twice.*

Tell

1 *Make a fist with your dominant hand, but stick out the index finger. Touch it to your chin.*

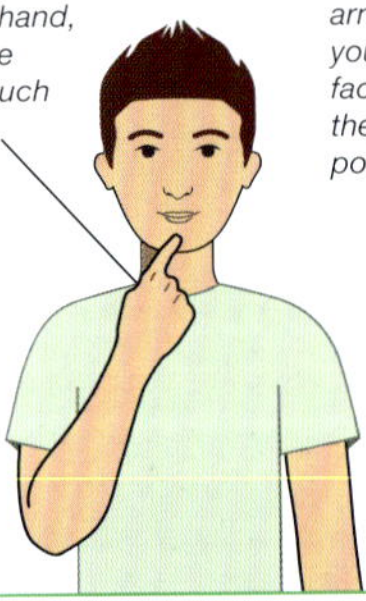

2 *Move your arm away from you, with the fist facing up and the index finger pointing outward.*

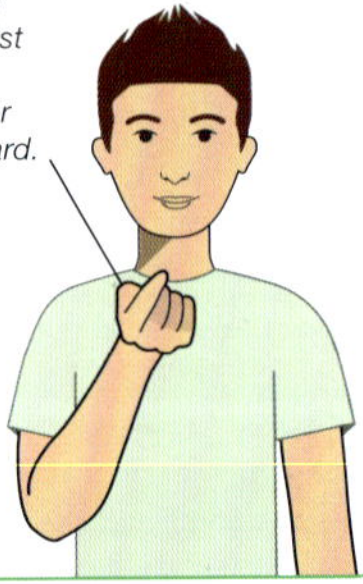

Shout

1 Curl your dominant hand inward into a claw shape, with the fingers slightly apart. Hold it in front of your mouth.

2 Open your mouth wide.

3 Tilt your head back, while squinting your eyes almost closed.

4 Move the hand up and away from you, toward your dominant side.

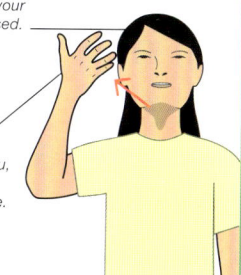

Whisper

1 Hold your dominant hand in front of your chin, with the fingers spread out, thumb folded in, and palm facing your nondominant side.

2 Wriggle your fingers softly as you lower your head.

TIP

To change the sign to "talk," tap your hand against your chin, twice, and stay upright while signing.

Forget

Left hand dominant

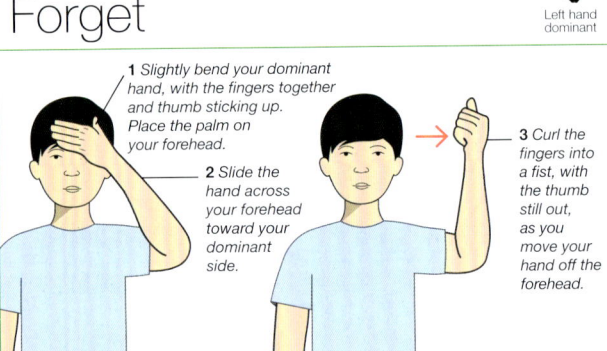

1 *Slightly bend your dominant hand, with the fingers together and thumb sticking up. Place the palm on your forehead.*

2 *Slide the hand across your forehead toward your dominant side.*

3 *Curl the fingers into a fist, with the thumb still out, as you move your hand off the forehead.*

Guess

1 *Curl your dominant hand into a loose "C" shape. Hold it by the side of your face, with the palm facing out.*

2 *Move your hand toward your nondominant shoulder, closing it into a fist as you move.*

Know

Bend your dominant hand, with the fingers together, and tap it against your forehead, twice.

Raise one eyebrow.

Think

Point the index finger of your dominant hand at the side of your head, with the other fingers curled into a fist.

Furrow your eyebrows and squint your eyes slightly.

Remember

1 *Curl your dominant hand into a fist, with your thumb stuck out and touching your forehead.*

2 *Curl your nondominant hand into a fist, with the thumb sticking up. Hold it near your chest.*

3 *Bring your dominant hand down until its thumb touches the thumb of your other hand.*

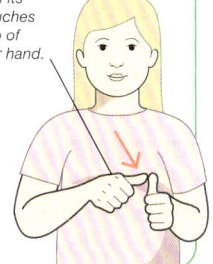

Understand

1 *Make a fist with your dominant hand, with the index finger touching your thumbnail, and the palm facing you.*

2 *Point your index finger upward, and nod your head.*

TIP

Shaking your head side to side can mean the opposite of a sign, so "don't understand" in this case.

Agree

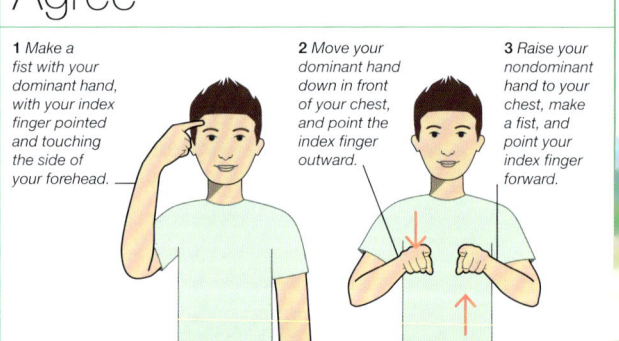

1 *Make a fist with your dominant hand, with your index finger pointed and touching the side of your forehead.*

2 *Move your dominant hand down in front of your chest, and point the index finger outward.*

3 *Raise your nondominant hand to your chest, make a fist, and point your index finger forward.*

Misunderstand

1 *Place your dominant hand at your forehead, with the palm facing up. Curl in your ring and little fingers.*

2 *Stick out your index and middle fingers, and place your thumb between them. Touch your index finger to your forehead.*

3 *Turn your hand over so that your middle finger touches your forehead.*

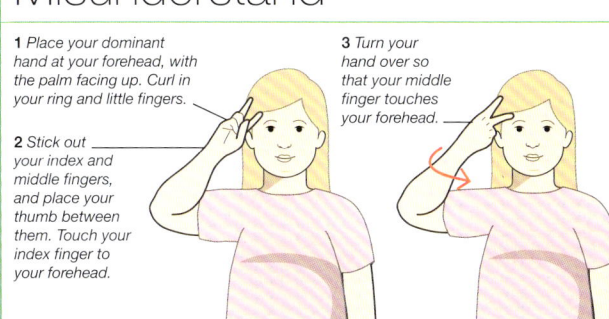

Disagree

1 *Make a fist with your dominant hand, with your index finger pointed and touching the side of your forehead.*

Slightly shake your head from side to side while signing.

3 *Move your hands outward, away from each other.*

2 *Hold your hands in front of your chest in fists, facing you, with the index fingers pointing at each other.*

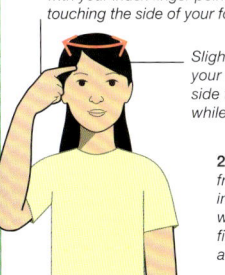

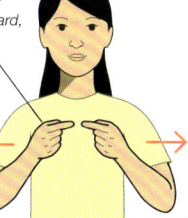

Can I help you?

This question can be used to sign "Can I help you?" or you can sign it toward yourself to ask "Can you help me?" To do this, replace "I" with "You" and "you" with "me" in the final step.

TIP

To sign "help," make the same handshape as in "help you," but move your hands upward.

Raise your eyebrows to show that you are asking a question.

1 *Make fists with both hands facing down.*

2 *Lower your hands to your waist.*

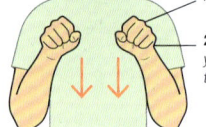

Can

3 *Point the index finger of your dominant hand at yourself while the other fingers remain curled in.*

5 *Make your dominant hand into a fist, with the thumb sticking up. Place this hand on your other hand.*

4 *Keep your nondominant hand flat in front of your chest, with the palm facing up.*

6 *Keep your hands in this position and move them forward in a straight line, toward the person you are addressing.*

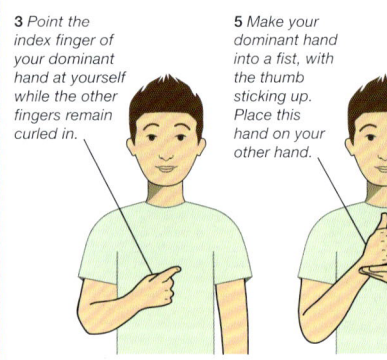

I   Help You

Can you feed the cat?

Raise your eyebrows.

1 *Make fists with both hands facing down.*

Can

2 *Lower your hands to your waist.*

3 *Make a fist with your dominant hand, and point your index finger at the person in front of you.*

You

4 *Pinch together the fingers and the thumb on both hands.*

5 *Hold your dominant hand near your mouth.*

Feed

6 *Keep your nondominant hand lower than your other hand and in front of it.*

7 *Move both hands forward and down a few times.*

8 *Bring both hands near your face. Spread the fingers and keep each index finger and thumb near your mouth.*

9 *Pinch the index finger and thumb together on each hand, pulling each one away from your face to the side, twice.*

Cat

Let's go to the ballpark.

We can sign "ballpark" by using the "baseball" sign, followed by fingerspelling the word "park."

TIP

To remember the sign for "baseball," imagine gently swinging an invisible baseball bat.

1 *Spread the fingers of your dominant hand, and hold it in front of your chest, with the palm facing you.*

Go

6 *Curl in your ring and little fingers. Point the middle finger toward you and the index finger and thumb up. Touch the base of your middle finger with your thumb.*

7 *Make your hand into a fist, with the palm facing away from you and the thumb on the outside of the fist.*

5 *Hold your dominant hand near your shoulder to fingerspell.*

The thumb touches the side of the middle finger.

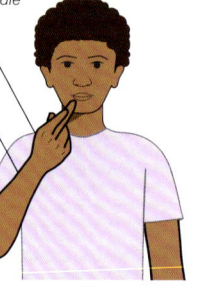

P

A

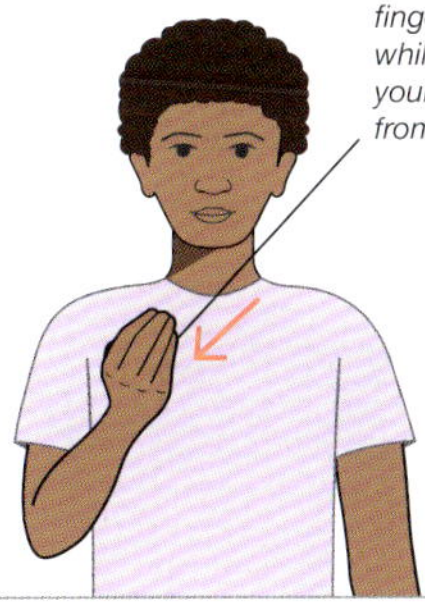

2 Bring your fingers together while pulling your hand away from you.

4 Keep your fists together and swing them a short distance away from you and then back, twice.

3 Make both hands into fists, and hold them in front of your dominant shoulder, with the dominant fist stacked on top of the other one.

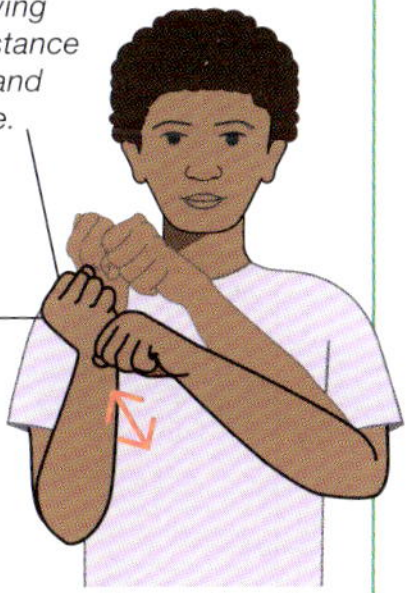

Baseball

8 Cross your index and middle fingers, and keep the thumb on top of the ring finger, with the other fingers curled in.

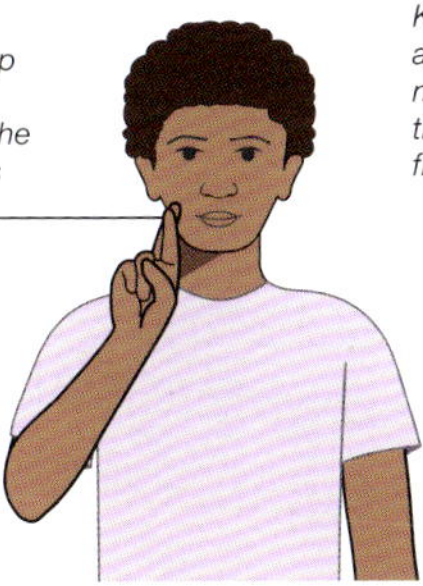

9 Point the index finger up and the middle finger diagonally up and toward your nondominant side. Keep the thumb at the base of the middle finger, with the ring and little fingers curled in.

R

K

Are you going swimming today?

It helps to imagine that you are really swimming when you are making the sign to swim.

Raise your eyebrows to show that you are asking a question.

2 Hold your hands in front of your chest, with the fingers facing in.

1 Curl your fingers into fists on both hands, but stick out the little fingers and thumbs to the sides.

Today

5 Make a fist with your dominant hand, but point the index finger at the person you are talking to.

You

TIP

To sign "swimming pool," just fingerspell the word "pool" after you sign "swimming."

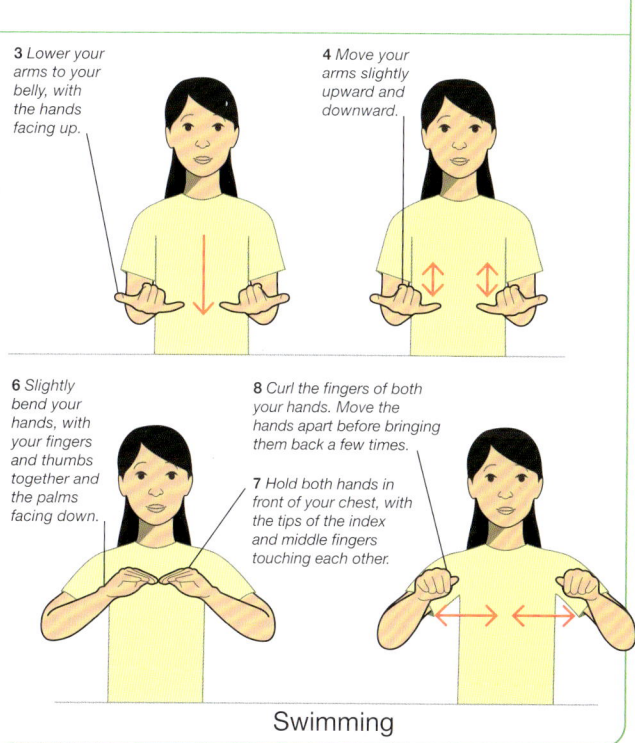

3 *Lower your arms to your belly, with the hands facing up.*

4 *Move your arms slightly upward and downward.*

6 *Slightly bend your hands, with your fingers and thumbs together and the palms facing down.*

8 *Curl the fingers of both your hands. Move the hands apart before bringing them back a few times.*

7 *Hold both hands in front of your chest, with the tips of the index and middle fingers touching each other.*

Swimming

I walk the dog before school.

2 *Place your dominant hand behind the other, with the fingers pointing sideways and the palm facing you. The back of this hand should touch the other one.*

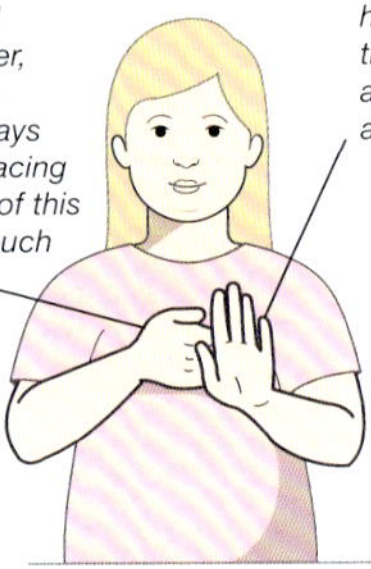

1 *Hold your nondominant hand in front of you, with the fingers pointing up and the palm facing away from you.*

3 *Move your dominant hand in, to rest on your chest.*

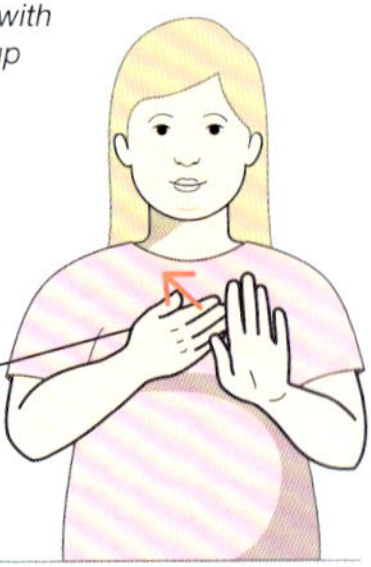

Before

7 *Point the index finger of your dominant hand at your chest, with the other fingers curled into a fist.*

8 *Bring your index finger and thumb together, as if you are holding a leash, keeping the other fingers curled in.*

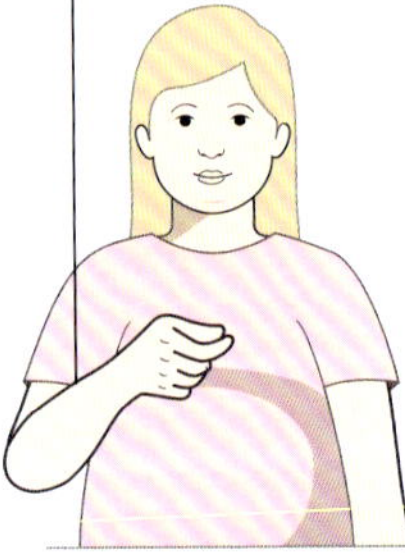

9 *Move your hand a little downward and away from you.*

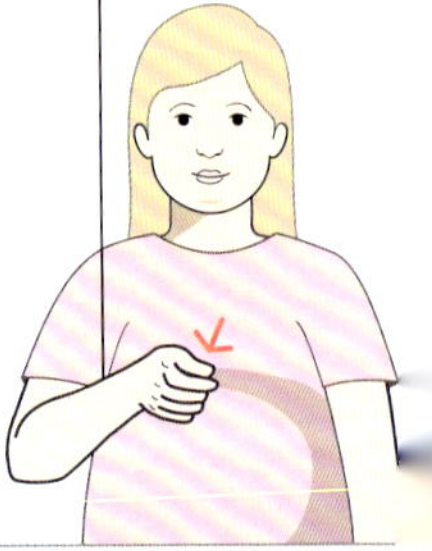

I

Walk

5 *Hold your dominant hand flat above your other hand, with the palm facing down.*

4 *Hold your nondominant hand in front of your chest, with the palm facing up.*

6 *Clap twice by moving your dominant hand down on the other hand.*

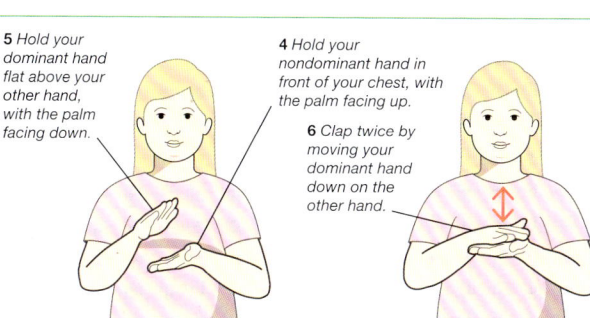

School

10 *Touch your middle finger to your thumb and stick out the index finger, while keeping the other fingers curled.*

11 *Snap your middle finger and thumb, twice, then bring your thumb near your index finger and fold in the middle finger too.*

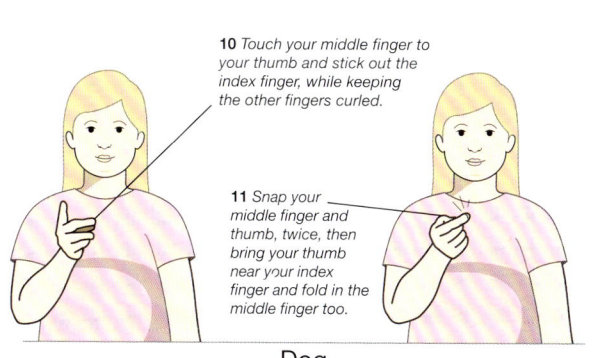

Dog

ASL alphabet

American Sign Language has its own alphabet. It is made up of 26 hand signs, one each for every letter of the English alphabet. If you don't know the sign for a particular word, you can use these signs to "fingerspell" it.

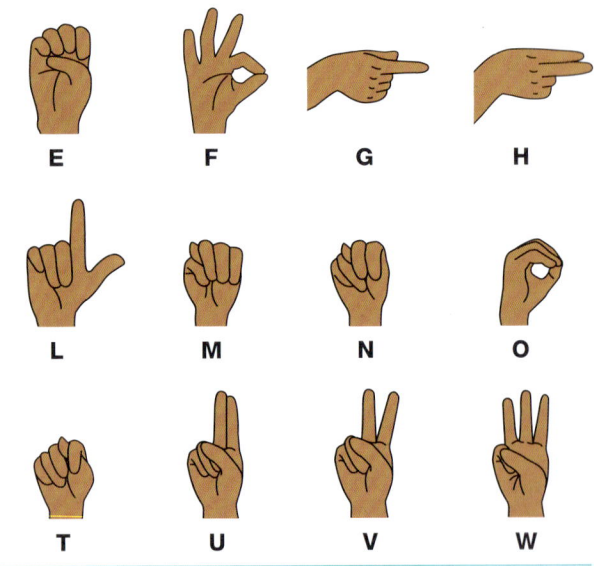

E F G H

L M N O

T U V W

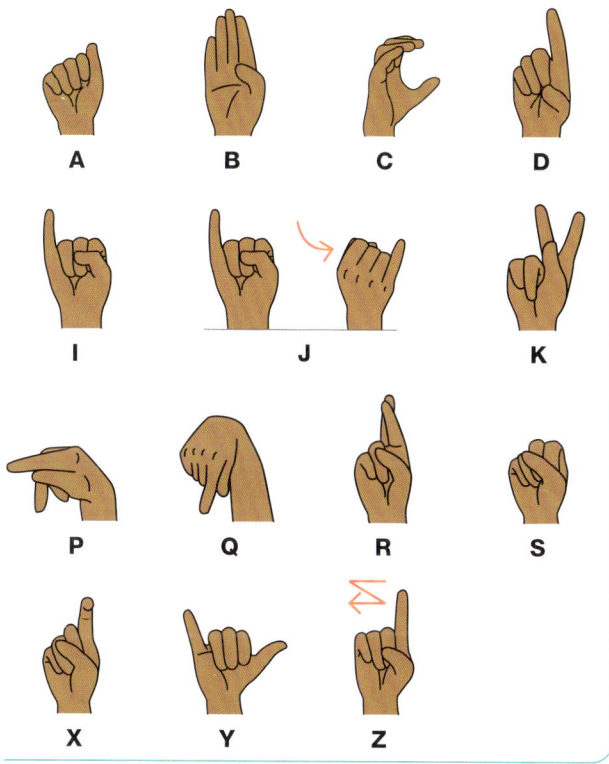

ASL numbers

American Sign Language has unique signs for all numbers. Some of these are given here. The signs can be used to "fingerspell" larger numbers using your dominant hand, or even to tell time.

0

1

2

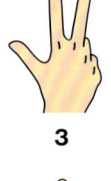

3

4

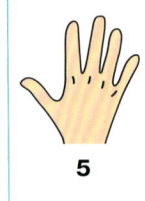

5

6

7

8

9

10

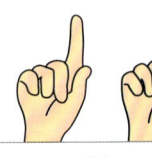

20

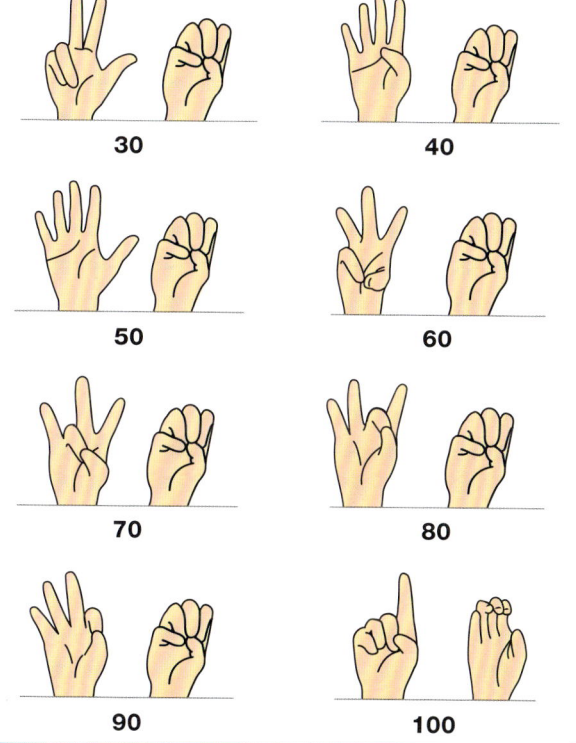

30

40

50

60

70

80

90

100

Glossary

Alternately
One and then the other. In ASL, one hand might need to be moved after the other for some signs.

Base hand
The nondominant hand may become an unmoving base for your dominant hand during two-handed signs.

Clockwise
Moving in the same direction as the hands of a clock.

Counterclockwise
Moving in the opposite direction to the hands of a clock.

Dominant hand
The hand a person prefers when doing activities. This is the hand a person might use most for signing in ASL.

Handshape
A particular shape made with the hands, especially in sign languages.

Hearing
Someone born with the ability to hear.

Interlock
To fit together.

Nondominant hand
The hand that a person might not like to use for activities. In ASL, this hand is used only for two-handed signs.

Sign
In ASL, a sign is a set of movements with a specific meaning.

Acknowledgments

The publisher would like to thank the following people for their help with making the book: Upamanyu Das, Zarak Rais, Rupa Rao, and Anna Streiffert Limerick for editorial assistance; Heena Sharma and Aparajita Sen for design assistance and making illustrations; Dheeraj Singh for DTP assistance; Lisa Jane Gillespie and the DK Inclusion and Impact team for a sensitivity check; Tessera Editorial for a sensitivity review of base illustrated characters; Dheeraj Arora and Romi Chakraborty for the jacket; Rituraj Singh for picture research assistance; and Chuck Hutchinson for proofreading.

The publisher would like to thank the following for their kind permission to reproduce their photographs:
(Key: a-above; b-below/bottom; c-center; f-far; l-left; r-right; t-top)

Cover images: *Front:* **Shutterstock.com:** Ground Picture bc.